THE GIRL IN THE MIDDLE

THE GIRL
IN THE
MIDDLE

GROWING UP BETWEEN BLACK AND WHITE,
RICH AND POOR

Anais Granofsky

HarperOne
An Imprint of HarperCollinsPublishers

HarperCollins books may be purchased for educational, business, or sales promotional use. For information, please email the Special Markets Department at SPsales@harpercollins.com.

FIRST EDITION

Designed by Alan Jones

Library of Congress Cataloging-in-Publication Data has been applied for.

ISBN 978-0-06-291463-7

22 23 24 25 26   LSC   10 9 8 7 6 5 4 3 2 1

To my children, Zadie, Toby and Walker

THE GIRL IN THE MIDDLE

Chapter One

YOU GO ON NOW, BABY GIRL." WE SAID GOODBYE quickly, my mother and me, clutching at each other, her urging me to go and me desperate to make her stay. Her long brown fingers and lean muscular arms wrapping around me; her small Afro tickling my nose as she whispered in my ear, "Be polite to these people."

These people. My father's people. I looked at my grandmother—my father's mother—sitting in her salmon-colored Cadillac that was pulled up to the curb, engine idling. I had only met her a few times, when I was an infant and then infrequently over the years when my father would take me to visit her without my mother. She was a stranger to me, this well-dressed white woman in an impossibly shiny vehicle. She stared straight ahead, looking embarrassed at the commotion I was making. She was perfectly put together, her coral lipstick applied evenly, hair meticulously styled in a chic and shiny bob that came to a curving end just below her ears. I fixed my gaze on a pair of glasses that hung from a slender gold chain around her neck. I saw her glance over at my mother, but the two women didn't speak.

My mother released me from her arms but held my hand tightly, the way she would when we passed drunks in the hallway of our rooming house, a tightening of the fingers and a hard pull to her hip when a fight broke out on the rough streets of our downtown neighborhood. To feel this now made me confused and scared. She was telling me to go but holding onto me the way she did when she was afraid. When she sensed danger. Unsure, I stood between her and my grandmother. Between worlds. Black and white. Rich and poor. My mother held me close one last time and then opened the car door and hustled me inside. Ragged running shoes on the pristine floor mat, the overpowering smell of fresh leather as my mom buckled me in. A whir and a metal snap. The two women never made eye contact. Never spoke. My mother put my bag at my feet and stepped back so that I had to strain to see her as my grandmother shifted the car into drive and pulled away. My old world retreating in the side mirror and a new world just beyond my view.

* * *

MY mother and I had just ridden a subway and two buses to get to the York Mills subway station in the north end of Toronto, where we met up with my grandmother. We had started the morning in our room at a flophouse near Dovercourt Road and College Street in Parkdale, a rough neighborhood on the west side of downtown Toronto. Parkdale was once a wealthy enclave glutted with large Victorian homes made of red brick from the legendary Don Valley Brick Works. The belching, massive brick factory manufactured the blocks that would help to build the city. Over the years, though, Parkdale had steadily fallen into disrepair and despair, and the once grand homes had been roughly divided into rooming houses.

In the house our room was in, most of the ornamental plaster detailing was gutted, the original stainglassed windows were shattered, the arched entrances boarded up. Garbage was always strewn in the hallways, and behind our door, a single mattress lay on the floor. My mother and I slept there together under a faded flower blanket. We had been in the rooming house for about two months, moving in after we could no longer afford the rent on the small apartment that had been our home for a year. In the mornings when addicts would shout through the thin walls, my mother would turn up the music and dance. Stalked by poverty and a pernicious insecurity, we turned to each other. That morning we had danced to Aretha Franklin over a breakfast of dry Froot

Loops, loud and silly to hide a nervous energy. She told me we were going "Way the hell up north to visit your grandma so we better get dressed up nice." Her behavior made me wary. I watched her closely but didn't say anything to tip the balance.

Things had been going from bad to worse for us and I had quickly learned that my own sadness and fear would not change anything. Would not help us. My mother was drowning and I was desperately trying to keep us afloat. I stayed attuned to her moods and tried not to upset her. Kept close at her side for fear that she might just slip away. So, I watched her put silver rings on her fingers and a patterned silk scarf in her hair. She threw on a wrap dress over bell-bottom jeans. I noticed she was checking herself in the mirror more than she usually did. She told me to put on my favorite frayed dress with the ruffles at the shoulders, the one that matched my maroon-colored socks. Taking a small bag, she packed it with my flannel pajamas, a *Laverne & Shirley* T-shirt, socks, underwear and my one-eyed bear. I diligently cleaned my scuffed sneakers with a wet rag and then put them on and tied them up. As I was rearranging my hair barrettes, she gave me a smile that was both bitter and determined. I hesitated at the door, anxious and trying to read her mood. "I don't want to go, Ma." She grabbed my hand and hustled me out. "Come on now, we gotta make the bus." We left our room and just made it to the stop as the bus was pulling up. We boarded, put our change in the fare box and began our long trip north. From gray to green. From need to opulence.

* * *

As my mother and her reassuring brown hands receded in the side mirror, my heart beat hard in my chest and I held back nervous tears. My grandmother reached over and patted my leg, telling me I should call her Shirley. I didn't look over and didn't say a word, my head spinning, the smell of fresh leather, warmed in the noon-day sun, making it hard to breathe. I knew that this woman was my grandmother, but I didn't know what that meant exactly. I vaguely remembered the visits when I was younger, but they had always been short and filled with tension and sometimes outright conflict. I remembered repeated arguments about our family needing money and the realization that my mother never came with us. Her unexplained absence was confusing and I always felt relieved when we left. But even those visits had stopped when my parents' tumultuous marriage fell apart and my father left.

It had been months and a couple of moves since we had heard from his family, so it had come as a surprise when my grandmother tracked us down. By then my mom and I were in trouble. Shirley found us and called to see me again, asking if I could come for an overnight weekend visit. My mother misheard and enthusiastically agreed to both of us coming up, grateful for a break from our tattered room. There was a long silence and in that silence it became clear that my mother was not invited to join me. Her pride wounded, she thought of hanging up. "Then I looked around me and I was tapped out and hurtin'. I didn't know if I could keep things together much longer. I thought they might have something to help you out, make life a little easier. So I swallowed my pride," she told me.

Now, riding together, I began to take Shirley in. In the way her hand rubbed my knee and the steady set of her jaw was something familiar. There was something of my dad in her and it made me miss him terribly. I hadn't seen him in months and my heart ached at his absence. I became angry at Shirley for not letting my mom come with us and angry at my dad for not being there. I couldn't understand all of the adult bitterness and unspoken rules, but I could feel them. She turned and assured me that "we're going to have a lovely time, Puja. You wipe your eyes. I've got lunch ready for us."

Puja. Only my dad still called me that. Heat bloomed in my chest and I felt the sting of tears rise up again. I could tell she was trying to make me feel better, but I just didn't know what she wanted from me. How was I supposed to behave with this woman? What was expected of me in this new world without either of my parents to guide me? We turned down a tree-lined street lousy with gated mansions and I stared out the window in amazement. Massive piles hidden discreetly behind tall green hedges. Stone turrets and huge picture windows flashing by.

The new car smell was increasingly making me motion sick. The white-leather interior, so pristine and smooth. Warm sweat beading down my back and rolling into my underwear. My stomach lurched and swayed as I tried desperately to keep my cereal down. Tingling in the back of my jaw and then the taste of bile. It was no use; I couldn't hold back any longer. Scrambling, I hastily rolled down the window and threw up mightily. A rainbow of Froot Loops arced out of the passenger-side window and splattered along the window behind. The colors, so vibrant in my cracked bowl that morning, had digested into a dark blue. My grandmother gave a quick intake of breath, no doubt shocked and slightly horrified. Without pulling over she handed me a cloth to wipe my mouth. I took it and noticed her initials stitched into it in green thread, with small flowers around the edges. SG. A fancy curlicue font that tapered to a single stitch. I had never seen letters so pretty and detailed. Refusing to get it dirty, I held onto it and wiped my mouth with the back of my hand instead. I laid my forehead against the glossy wood-grain paneling on the door, the cool breeze from outside blowing my sweaty curls, making me feel better. Taking a deep, shaky breath, I held the pretty cloth in my damp grip. Tracing those stitched letters with the tip of my thumb made me feel steadier. *SG.* They were my father's initials too.

It reminded me that I was connected to him and so was she and it settled my nerves. I looked up as we eventually turned off the road and onto a smooth driveway, the sound of the rubber wheels changing, becoming softer, soothing.

I gazed wide-eyed as we drove by a fountain misting water across an emerald-green lawn. The thick carpet of grass in an endless, undulating conformity. Tall trees framed the entrance to the house, while clipped, angular hedges lined the drive. A tennis court and swimming pool were just visible in the back garden, with its flowers in bloom and green hills leading to a blue-sky horizon. I had never noticed the horizon before; in the cramped quarters where we lived it appeared only broken and fleeting as you chased it around the corner of a building. Here it was unmistakable, so clean and true and uninterrupted. We pulled up to the top of the circular driveway and stopped in front of a red-brick colonial mansion with a grand front entrance and white columns. The house had wide double doors, and the many double-hung windows were flanked by white shutters. A three-car garage stood to one side and a thicket of willow trees to the other. The trees' long-hanging branches, thick and full, sweeping the ground.

My grandmother parked the car and cut the engine, the sound of birds and distant lawn mowers rushing in to fill the silence. The pungent smell of cut grass. My grandmother turned to me; she seemed about to say something but then thought better of it. She opened her car door and stepped out, smoothing her knee-length skirt and silk blouse. I sat there, unmoving, until my grandmother had to come and carefully work around the vomit to open my door. She gently coaxed me out of the car, taking my hand as I grabbed my bag and reluctantly slid down from the seat. We walked up the front steps and through the wide double doors. My scuffed running shoes and uneven socks, hand clutching my bag as I walked across the threshold. The door closed behind us, the interior so cool and hermetically sealed it took a moment for my senses to adjust. The front entrance was dominated by a curving staircase and a crystal chandelier. Teardrops of cut glass twinkling in the muted light. Fresh-cut flowers in a blue-and-white porcelain bowl sat lush and full on a delicate table. Framed drawings of birds lined the wall, intricately sketched creatures on a tree branch. Unused candles in gold candelabras were reflected in a gilded mirror above an antique wooden dresser where Shirley set her purse and keys. I caught a glimpse of myself as we passed by it, eyes wide, hair wild and curly and slightly disheveled. Even to myself I looked out of place.

We continued through the foyer and past room after room of silent, stifling affluence. A dining table long enough to seat eighteen with another crystal chandelier hanging above it, this one smaller but no less ornate. Velvet-backed dining chairs fronted thick flowered wallpaper above carved wooden wainscotting. Eventually we entered the living room, where my grandmother stopped. "Why don't you sit down and wait while I quickly get us our lunch?" I glanced over at the stiff, pillow-filled couch, and when she saw that there was no way in hell I was going to sit down, she nodded and left. I stood motionless, overwhelmed by the lavish space. Silk brocade curtains framed the picture windows that overlooked the lush gardens I had glimpsed when we arrived. A large painting of a pastoral country scene hung above the fireplace; I would later learn it was of a rural shtetl in Eastern Europe with hay bales and gloaming skies. There were tchotchkes and awards from Jewish organizations crowding the mantles: *Phil and Shirley Granofsky for their contributions . . .* , etc. I was fascinated by the Star of David on one business award, and a scroll of Hebrew text written in gold calligraphy. I knew my dad's family was Jewish but no one had ever explained what that meant. Was I Jewish? I had no idea.

Curious, I was drawn to a marble table top that held black-and-white photos of old-fashioned men sitting for their portrait in ill-fitting woolen suits and full beards. The women standing behind them wore headscarves, long, thick skirts and exhausted expressions of despair and fortitude. I vaguely remembered stories my dad had told me about grandparents who were immigrants and had crossed oceans. Relatives from the "old country." I quietly searched for a trace of myself in their pale, ancient faces and found none.

★ ★ ★

WE sat by the sparkling pool and ate a lunch of chicken salad sandwiches and iced tea. I had never had a chicken salad sandwich before but it immediately became my new favorite food in the world. Thick with mayonnaise, it had small half-moons of celery in it and was served on buttered challah bread. The ice tea sweet and fresh. I looked around, eating hungrily, and realized that this wasn't so bad. I tried to focus on Shirley, who chatted softly, still trying to put me at ease, but I couldn't stop looking at my surroundings. Especially the pool; it was mesmerizing. The sun reflecting off the long, perfect rectangle of crystal blue. I had never seen a pool that wasn't public and thronging with the huddled masses. I didn't even know people had private pools. I hadn't seen it on my previous visits and was thrilled to find it now. I looked around, chewing and taking every detail in, from the pool chairs with yellow-and-white-striped slats that were casually lined up around the stone decking area to the plush towels that had been neatly folded and piled in a basket for use. They even had a telephone outside! A bright canary-yellow top-handle with a clear circular dial that was propped on its own small plastic table. Its magic given away only slightly by a long cord disappearing into the kitchen's open sliding glass doors. Bright red hydrangeas sat in outdoor pots at measured intervals along the black wrought iron fence that separated the pool from the endless

curving hills that made up the rest of the manicured property. The opulence and grandeur inside the house had been
too overwhelming and stifling for me, but out here by the
blue pool eating lunch it was . . . beautiful. As I drank the
last of the tea, I heard the ice cubes clinking in the bottom
of my glass, again smelled that pungent scent of freshly cut
grass. I closed my eyes, took in the warm breeze and slowly
felt something unknot in my chest. The quiet beauty and
ease somehow reassured me. Finally, I let my guard down,
only then realizing how heavy it had been.

* * *

THAT night I slept in my aunt's childhood room, on the
second floor at the top of the wide staircase. Before bed I
changed into my old pajamas and took my one eyed-bear
out of my bag. The bedroom had a white four-poster bed
with a canopy that had scalloped edges and a braided gold
trim. I hopped up on the high mattress that was made up
with thick blankets and rows of pillows, tassels at their crisp
corners. The bed was tucked so efficiently and tightly it was
hard for me to wiggle my feet under the blankets as I was
getting in.

My dad's youngest sister, Maxine, had left for college
that year, leaving the house empty for the first time. With
all four of her children out of the house, either married,
traveling or at school, and her husband working long hours,

my grandmother had an unusual amount of time on her hands. She knocked at the door and then came in and stood just inside the room, glancing around. "I haven't been in here in a while. It seems like I don't even use half the house now that everyone's gone." She noticed my clothes on the floor and picked them up with the tips of her fingers, holding them slightly away from her as she folded them into a dresser drawer. "I thought tomorrow we could go shopping and pick you up a few things. Something pretty to wear." I nodded silently. She stood there awkwardly while I tried to think of something to say. Tried to figure out how to thank her for lunch; thank her for the sparkling pool and the quiet afternoon and the unlocked feeling in my chest. But I didn't know where to begin. "Alright. I'll see you in the morning, dear. If you need anything, I'm just down the hall." She turned off the light and left, leaving the door slightly ajar.

I lay back into the stiff pillows and looked across the dim room. A collection of beautiful porcelain dolls stood sentry on a shelving unit painted pink. The dolls wore silk dresses and knee-high socks, and their shiny hair in ribbons. They were the kind that closed their eyes when you laid them down. I was both enamored with and terrified of their blank stares and perfect clothes. I looked down at my beloved bear with her bald fur and hanging-button eye and realized for the first time how pathetic she was. I stuffed her under the blankets and rolled over. The sliver of hallway I could see was wide and dark and full of silence. I was so used to noise and music and sometimes shouting through the night that this muted silence was strangely deafening. I suddenly felt exposed so high off the floor in such a big bed without my mom. I was used to the company of her warm body on a thin mattress just off a wooden floor. I quickly crawled down from the thick bed and laid my cheek against the wall-to-wall carpet lined with vacuum marks. It felt better down here. Everything smelled so clean and new. Pulling down a pillow and a throw blanket, I wrapped myself up and exhaled. My grandmother found me asleep on the floor in the morning.

★ ★ ★

THE next day, Shirley and I got ready to go shopping for new clothes. At breakfast she explained that I would keep the clothes at their place. "We're going to buy you some proper clothes for when you visit. They won't be for out in the streets. We'll keep them clean and safe here for you."

After running an errand to the kosher butcher, we stopped at a "young miss" shop in a strip mall near their home. The small bell at the top of the door chimed as we walked in, and classical music played softly over the speakers. The woman behind the front desk walked over, plastering a smile across her jaw as she saw my grandmother, beautifully dressed and styled. Her smile slipped on its hinges slightly when she got a look at me. A little Black girl holding her grandmother's hand, a *Laverne & Shirley* T-shirt and lopsided socks completing the incongruous picture. My grandmother ignored her look of confusion. "I'd like to see a couple different outfits for my granddaughter. We're going to need shoes and socks as well." The saleswoman quickly led us into the store, pointing out options as we went. Lagging behind, I ran my hand along the rows of lace-trimmed dresses with velvet sashes. Rows of shiny patent-leather Mary Jane shoes propped up in their boxes. They reminded me of the clothes on the scary dolls back in my aunt's room.

My grandmother called me over as the saleswoman stood at a change-room door with an armful of clothes and an expectant smile. I hesitated and then went inside and begrudgingly began to try a few things on. I liked my scuffed running shoes and cut-off jean shorts; I didn't know why anything had to change. But then, as I began to get dressed, I marvelled at my reflection in the dull light of the change-room mirror. I looked so . . . fancy. It made me think of my mom and I tried not to like it too much. We bought two of the dresses, a more casual skirt and top, two pairs of new shoes, a nightdress and a coat. When we returned to the house we hung the dresses in the closet of my aunt's room and lined up the new shoes. I changed into the skirt and top and my old clothes were washed, folded and put into a plastic bag that was stored away in the back of the dresser.

That day, I kept catching glimpses of myself in the mirrors around the house and it surprised me every time. My grandmother had efficiently put my hair up in a neat bun, and the clothes were so new and clean. At home my mother always liked my hair wild and messy, and my clothes were bought at the local Salvation Army. This put-together kid gave me a secret thrill. She looked like she belonged in that reflection. All day I kept surreptitiously returning to the closet to check on the dresses, looking over the velvet sashes and delicate ruffles. Thrilled at the glittering newness of it all, I tried not to think of the plastic bag tucked away in the drawer, its contents a reminder of the situation that was waiting for me at home. I instinctively knew I could never tell my mother about the new clothes. It wasn't a decision that I made—it didn't even feel like a choice. Enjoying the clothes and, worse, my time with Shirley was, I knew, a betrayal of my mother. I realized that I was going to have to leave this new reflection of myself at my grandmother's house along with the dresses hanging in the closet. As I stood there, I wouldn't admit even to myself how happy I felt away from the grinding pressure of our poverty.

The next morning, Shirley and I had a swim in the pool and fruit cups out on the patio. Then I changed into my old clothes and we left the house. When we got in the car, Shirley handed me a plastic bag with a raised eyebrow. The smell of the car's interior already making me feel a bit queasy, I gratefully accepted it and felt in my pocket for the delicate hanky I had kept. She started the car and we made the long, winding trip back downtown. From green to gray. The wide-open sky slowly swallowed up by concrete.

Eventually we pulled up in front of our building, and Shirley sat staring when she realized where we were living. I was excited and surprisingly relieved to be home and to be getting out of the hot car with my breakfast intact. Although I had come to enjoy my time with Shirley, this was home. I quickly opened the door. "Thank you, Shirley!" She smiled and clasped my hand before I could make a run for it. One running shoe on the broken cement, the other on the pristine floor mat. "I'm going to ask your mother if I can take you again next weekend," she said. "Is that okay with you?" I thought about my mother, and then nodded. She leaned over and kissed me on the cheek before I finished my escape from the car.

Running into the building I stopped suddenly, remembering my hair was in a neat bun. I quickly pulled the elastic out and gave my head a hard shake, roughing up my hair and letting the curls fall out into a messy halo. I untucked my *Laverne & Shirley* shirt and wrinkled the smooth material. Then I sprinted up the stairs two at a time and burst into our room. My mother stood at the window watching Shirley's car pull away. I couldn't read her expression exactly, but I knew it wasn't good. So I ran over and hugged her hard and to my relief she smiled. She bent down and her smile faltered slightly as she spotted Shirley's lipstick kiss on my cheek. Reaching out she roughly wiped it away, asking grimly, "Was it fun?" I shook my head. "I hated it, Ma. It was awful." Her smile returned, the sun from behind the clouds, and she hugged me back. A few days later, Shirley called again, and even though I pretended to be unwilling, another weekend visit was arranged.

★ ★ ★

OVER the next few years, we fell into a routine. Every couple of weeks, my mother and I would travel from our low-income apartment downtown up to the York Mills subway stop and get on a bus. At the bus stop, my grandmother would pick me up in her pink Cadillac and take me to their house for a weekend or one of the Jewish holidays. I was constantly traveling between two worlds, bouncing between the realms of wealth and need, ease and strife, Jewishness and Blackness, childhood and maturity. I felt guilty leaving my mother behind, struggling, but after establishing the rules early, we never spoke about my visits with Shirley. As the years went on, I told my mother less and less about the other world I inhabited. I always looked forward to my time with Shirley, but her world was also a complicated one to navigate as a little Black girl. I hid my life back home from my grandmother as well, feeling as if it would be disrespectful to my mother to speak about her with someone she seemed to hate. Shirley made it easy by very rarely inquiring and often showing disdain when I did let something slip. I felt protective of both of them and didn't want to hear them speaking badly about one another. Their continued estrangement lead to a tacit and complicated agreement with both women to never speak of the other life I was living. To survive, I learned to switch who I was in these radically different worlds. It became second nature to cleave myself in two.

Chapter Two

THIS IS THE STORY OF MY GRANDMOTHER, MY MOTHER and myself. Rich and poor. Black and white. Three generations of women. One family. It's the story of race, class, hatred, bigotry, love and, ultimately, redemption. Our story of beauty and grace through generations of despair. My ancestors came from opposite sides of the world and, like so many refugees, struggled to find their way in a hostile new land. In turn, their children also desired a new life, themselves only several generations out of American slavery and Europe's pogroms. My father's family thrived, moving up the class ladder and becoming an example of the immigrant Canadian promise. My mother's family loved one another deeply but each of them stagnated, struggling to find their way out of a system of violence and poverty in rural America. My parents reached across a chasm of culture, race, religion and life experience to have a child that would inhabit all of these worlds. A girl in the middle of history, migration and chance encounters.

* * *

My mother, Jean, was the thirteenth child of fifteen, born in 1949 to a church-going Black family in Cedarville, Ohio. They lived on a forty-acre farm where they grew corn and green beans and raised a few animals. The farm's broken stone path heaved and shattered over the roots of a massive Ohio buckeye that dominated the hardscrabble yard. A rubber truck tire swinging from a frayed rope tied to one of its long, reaching branches. The tire had been made just down the road in the town of Akron, Ohio— *Rubber Capital of the World!* faded into its pitted and balding treads. The worn, two-bedroom farmhouse sat high on a gentle bend in the hill, surrounded by working fields and dirt roads that disappeared into the warm, shimmering haze. Its siding was a moss-green color, paint chipped and flaked. Yellowing Chantilly lace curtains hung limply in the window as if trying to conjure a more genteel time. The smell of cottonwood and sassafras pungent in the humid air.

* * *

THE farm belonged to my grandmother, Doreen Peterson, inherited from her parents and brought into her marriage to Alonzo Walker. Just three generations out of slavery, my grandmother's maternal people were descended from the famous "Randolph slaves." John Randolph was a slaveholder and a scion of the most powerful family in the American South from the late 1700s to the Civil War. His cousin was Thomas Jefferson and they would infrequently correspond, debating farming practices and the great themes of the day. He was the hugely wealthy master of a string of tobacco plantations in Virginia. But Randolph had always doubted the morality of slavery. On his death, after a long and debauched struggle with an opium addiction, he granted freedom to all of his slaves. This radical act enraged his fellow slaveholders and set off a vicious court battle with his heirs. But the will was eventually ruled valid, and on June 10, 1846, the newly freed slaves, numbering 383, left Virginia.

John Randolph had stipulated that his former slaves be allowed to settle on a large uninhabited tract of land that he owned in Ohio, so the caravan headed north. Some had horses, but most walked the arduous five-hundred-mile journey to what they were convinced was the promised land. But Ohio was anything but welcoming. The freed men, women and children, including my great-great-grandfather, had to fight off marauders and barbarous whites who resented the newly arrived freed people.

Through sheer force of will, they eventually managed to build farmhouses on the willed plot of land and work the fertile fields through generations of violence and Jim Crow law. My grandmother Doreen was born into that same farmhouse and lived in its confines her whole life.

* * *

THE Walker men on my mother's paternal side—Alonzo's father and uncles—worked as porters at the Pennsylvania Railroad Company, a train route that traveled from Chicago through Ohio and on to New York. They mainly worked the sleeping cars on the Ohio route: from Toledo through to Fort Wayne, and on to Cincinnati, Columbus and Cleveland. They were part of the legendary generation of all-Black sleeping car porters. In the 1860s, American engineer and business man George Pullman pioneered the sleeping car. Traveling the vast railroads of the time was a hard-backed, sleepless and cramped affair. Pullman invented and built sleeping cars, lavish art-deco rolling hotels that served a high-end, white traveler. Pullman also hired newly freed slaves to work as porters on his sleeping cars. Pennsylvania Railroad followed suit; my great-grandfather was one of those men. The work was grueling and often demeaning. Porters were expected to be on call twenty-four hours a day, obsequious and grindingly deferential. But they became icons in the Black community. Dapper and proud, they provided economic stability to their families and communities. Lifting a whole generation up and establishing a Black middle class through their sweat and perseverance. Unlike most of their peers, porters had often traveled widely, many having seen different cities and states, some having traveled from coast to coast.

As a young man, my grandfather, Alonzo Walker, also had dreams of working the railroad and traveling the country like his father had before him. Alonzo was a sharp dresser who had a quick, easy wit and charm. As a teenager, he didn't like working too hard, so he eventually gave up on training for the railroad and instead got a day job at the Wright-Patterson Air Force Base. He spent his days driving munitions from one end of the massive military base to the other. This left his nights free to gamble, carouse and chase women. One Saturday evening before heading out for the night, Alonzo went with his cousins to watch a women's softball game down the road in Xenia. Doreen was her team's second baseman, and when she stepped up to bat, Alonzo told his cousin, "I'm gonna marry that girl." When he tried to sweet talk her after the game, she told him, "You better not let my daddy see you sniffing around." Undeterred, he began to court the younger woman. Alonzo was twenty-one and Doreen was sixteen.

Doreen's father, Maurice, a preacher, and his wife, Zadie, hated the older, fast-talking huckster in the three-piece suit. Doreen had been her senior class valedictorian and had dreams as big as a pretty colored girl in Ohio could have. She had been accepted into college to study home economics and she hoped to be a teacher someday. She was set to attend Wilberforce University in the fall of 1927, and her parents eagerly began to pack her off in the hopes of ending the budding romance. She never made it. The day Doreen was supposed to leave, she and Alonzo were secretly married after she discovered that she was pregnant with the first of what would be fifteen children. Alonzo took a more permanent full-time position at the air force base to support their growing family, and Doreen began cleaning the homes of wealthy white families in town. Alonzo soon went back to his womanizing and gambling while Doreen, heavily pregnant for many years, slowly came to rue the day he had seen her at that baseball game.

★ ★ ★

Doreen was the only one of three sisters to have children, so she inherited the farm when her parents died. The farm-house had only two bedrooms, and my mother's seven brothers slept in one bedroom while the eight sisters shared the other. Doreen and Alonzo slept on a pull-out bed on the screened-in porch in the summer. And in the winter, they slept in the living room, where a small bed was neatly made up in the corner near a wood-burning stove. By the time my mother was born, the house was chaotic, loud and filled to the rafters. The younger kids were watched by the older siblings while both parents worked. Doreen cleaned house for the same two families for decades. She would leave for work well before dawn and often came home after dark. She was always exhausted, and overrun the second she walked in the door. But her work along with Alonzo's salary—when she could get to it before he spent it on the weekend's entertainment—were enough to keep everyone fed and the roof over their heads.

The local Wright-Patterson Air Force Base complex outside of Dayton provided jobs for many of the Black men and women in their working-class town. Wright-Patterson was famous for being the location where Wilbur and Orville Wright perfected flying after their initial flights at Kitty Hawk. It was a massive complex of more than six hundred buildings spread out over eight thousand acres, where live and deactivated munitions had to be transported from one location to another. Alonzo worked there his entire adult life, transporting temperamental explosives on the bumpy backroads of the base. While driving the old bomb transport trucks, Alonzo was known to sit on his helmet in case something blew on the ride. He said, "I'd rather lose my head than my balls." After work, Alonzo was a charming and inveterate gambler who became known for the rowdy Saturday night juke joints he hosted at a neighbor's barn deep in the back fields. Lanterns lit and hanging from the rafters and music filling the dark night signaled to Black partygoers across the county that it was on. Inside, brown liquor was bottled and served from a backroom distillery built by Alonzo and his cousins from leftover gear they swiped from the base. Sometimes you could taste traces of the diesel fuel that hadn't been properly washed off the distillery parts in the whiskey and bourbon. Dice and card games were set up at one end of the barn and the band and dance floor at the other. The music, laughter and dancing were a sweaty exultation to the gods. A yearning to live free that my mother could hear from her bedroom window at night, Doreen long asleep in the small bed on the screened-in porch.

On Sunday morning, as the sun came up, Alonzo would return home and find his God-fearing wife getting ready for church. Doreen and Alonzo would fight bitterly over his no-account ways and wasteful spending. Doreen, who had become more and more religious over the years, would preach to her husband about sin and God's good grace. Alonzo, who had never been a religious man, would shoo her away and stumble off to fall into a deep, drunken slumber. While Alonzo slept, she would have to rifle through his pockets to claim whatever winnings he might have made, eventually coming away with a few creased and crumpled bills. Doreen would then march her huge brood down to the one-room Black church at the edge of town. They would file in noisily, taking up several pews down front along with Doreen's two childless sisters, who would smack the kids upside the head if they started acting out. My mother would sit straight-backed and attentive, not because she was a true believer, but because she enjoyed the music and spectacle of the preacher and choir. She was a thoughtful, curious kid, and early on she had begun to question the patriarchy and racism behind the worshipping of a white male Jesus in an all-Black, mostly female church. But she loved her family's Sunday mornings, first to worship and then home with cousins and neighbors for a breakfast of fried ham, eggs, pancakes and fresh milk. So, she sang at the top of her lungs and kept her theological doubts to herself.

★ ★ ★

Doreen and Alonzo would continue to grow in diametrically opposed ways over time, her religiosity keeping step with his debauchery. As they aged, she grew thick and low to the ground, while her husband stayed rake thin and over six feet tall. She wore compression stockings and sensible shoes, an apron layered over a modest shift dress that never rose above the knee. Alonzo famously remained known for his sharp suits and a hat always worn at a jaunty angle. He continued late in life to enjoy a good cigar, brown liquor and beautiful women. Doreen would become consumed by Jesus, her unending pregnancies and the ceaseless struggle to keep that many children fed.

The Walker children attended a small schoolhouse where the white kids sat up front and the Black students at the back, a row of empty desks between them. My mother, Jean, loved school and sat as close to the front of the Black section as she could, straining to catch every lesson, trying to hear every question she was never called on to answer. When she wasn't studying, Jean did chores around the farm. The girls planted the vegetable garden with corn and green beans, churned butter, did laundry, and took care of the younger children. Bedsheets fluttering in the breeze on the line, sisters chasing each other's shadows thrown into sharp relief by the sun. The smell of homemade laundry detergent; lavender and lye on the sheets. The boys helped with the heavy work and looked after the few animals they kept. They would gather at sunset to play baseball with a stick and ball or wrestle in the fields while the cows looked on. While there was a roof over their heads, there was hardly enough food or money to go around. But the family didn't feel poor. Everyone around them was in the same situation. The Walker family grew to be eight girls and seven boys: Mary-Anne, Bernice, Charlene, Judy, Rose, Kathleen, Joann and Jean; and Bud, John, Paul, Richard, Thomas, Lawrence and Martin, the baby of the family.

The older sisters and brothers were already in high school by the time my mother and her identical twin, Joann, were born. The older children were expected to watch the younger siblings while their parents worked, and the house was often anarchic. My mother was a sensitive girl who used to lie in the front yard and watch the clouds scuttle by. When my mother was young, her family doctor told her she had a blood condition that would likely prevent her from having children. She had always bruised easily and was prone to nosebleeds. Her brothers and sisters often played sports in the back field after school. Dropping books in the dusty fields of sassafras and corn, the older boys would organize a schoolyard pick for teams. Jean was always the last chosen, as she would inevitably end her game with bruised shins or gushing blood out of her nose. Her siblings scattering when the bleeding started so they weren't blamed for "making Jeanie bleed again!" They knew if someone was found to have been too rough with her it would lead to a whipping.

Eventually, Jean was banned from playing sports and spent her afternoons alone reading and doing housework inside. She could hear the crack of the ball and the shouts of her siblings running and playing out in the sunshine. As a child she had always felt defective, and she lived with a gnawing sadness that made her retreat into herself. This separation from her siblings and feeling of alienation continued to grow more acute over time. On one of her quiet wanderings, she found a cubbyhole in the back of a closet. It was behind a loose board that led to a small space between the walls where Jean would hide out and devour library books by the light of a bare bulb. No one could find her there, and she would often fall asleep forgotten. Waking up the next morning, she would crawl out of the closet to get ready for school, only her older sister Bernice having noticed she was gone or had just now reappeared.

Bernice, Jean's second-oldest sister, was something of a sister/mother to the twins when they were young. She would often save Jean a bowl of oatmeal and leave it for her at the cubby door so she would get breakfast. But once Bernice moved out, even that small attention disappeared. The cubby became a space of Jean's own, where she could escape her rowdy siblings and her parents' whippings. Jean was terrified of her parents' violence and felt completely different from her brothers and sisters. Book smart and tender, she was never fully comfortable around her robustly physical siblings. The older ones already half grown, the younger ones essentially left to fight for themselves. Her one true ally was her twin sister, Joann.

* * *

JEAN and Joann were the last girls born and the second-to-last children in the family. There were nine years between the next-youngest sister, Kathleen, and them. So, Jean and Joann were all each other had.

The twins were physically identical while being wildly opposed in personality. While Jean was quiet and studious, Joann was adventurous and outgoing. In high school, Jean was a loner who spent most of her time reading and doing homework at the library. One time, she checked out *The Three Musketeers*, found a spot in the corner of the library and disappeared into the swashbuckling tale. When she looked up the lights had been turned off and the front door was locked. She had to climb out of the bathroom window and make her way home. Joann, on the other hand, rolled with a large group of friends and spent most of her time in high school partying. She would sneak out late at night and come tumbling back through the window early in the morning as Jean was getting ready for school. Jean was always mistaken for Joann: on the street men would lean out of cars and call her sister's name. Joann's friends would run up to her before realizing they had the wrong twin and awkwardly make an excuse to move on. But Joann was protective of Jean and would menace anyone who dared pick on her cerebral twin. Although they were radically different, they were protective of each other.

Jean worked tirelessly throughout high school to get away from her crowded, rural home life. Doreen encouraged her children to get an education, and she was proud of her youngest daughter's academic accomplishments, perhaps recognizing her own long-ago dreams of becoming a teacher. But my mother was far too low on the family food chain to get much attention. The only time my mother remembers her parents sitting down with the family was on April 4, 1968. The night Martin Luther King Jr. was assassinated.

The entire family gathered in front of the television set to watch the news. Jean remembers her mother quietly weeping into her apron and her older siblings standing shocked in the kitchen. Shortly after, and still reeling from that traumatic event, Jean was told by her school guidance counselor that despite her excellent marks she shouldn't bother applying to college and would most likely have to follow her mother into domestic service. Jean left that meeting furious and fighting back tears. Having just seen her civil rights hero murdered, she vowed then that she would never let anyone stop her from getting out. As her twin Joann dated and partied, my mother studied relentlessly. She also became more political, writing articles about equal rights that her school newspaper refused to publish. Black kids were still not allowed on the school student council, in the theater productions or on the cheerleading squad. So, Jean staged a walk-out to protest these injustices, but she was the only one who showed up. Joann finally took pity on her sister and forced her large group of friends to join Jean, fists raised, chanting "We want in!"

By the end of Jean's senior year, she had fought for and earned a federal scholarship for colored students that would allow her to apply to Antioch College in Yellow Springs, Ohio. Antioch was a liberal arts college and one of the first postsecondary schools to integrate; as an equal rights advocate and a nascent feminist, Jean was drawn to Antioch's progressive vibe. In 1971, she was accepted into the women's studies and journalism program. Her parents didn't know where they were going to find the money to pay for what her scholarship didn't cover, but they promised her they would do what they could. In the spring of that year Joann revealed to Jean that she was pregnant. Too afraid to tell anyone else, Joann also admitted that she had decided to drop out of high school to do what she could to prepare for the baby.

"You oughta finish up, Joann," my mother pleaded late at night on the front porch of the farm as the scent of flowering crab apple hung in the air. "You're not going to have no way to get out of here otherwise."

"Getting out is your thing, Jeanie, not mine. I'll find my own damn way. You might know a lot, but you don't know everything."

Jean hugged her sister and touched her new belly curiously, reminded of her own inability to get pregnant. It felt to her like both a blessing and a curse. "Who's the daddy?"

Joann rolled her eyes. "Some boy up near Dayton way. Said he was happy, wanted to take care of me."

Jean shook her head. "I hope he does."

The twin girls sat holding each other as their paths radically diverged ahead of them.

Late that summer, when their parents found out Joann was pregnant, they were furious and told her they "would not be responsible for another mouth to feed." By this time most of their fifteen children were grown and out of the house, and they were finally looking forward to having a little bit of money to fix up their home. The entire family had used an outhouse for years, and Doreen dreamed of having an indoor toilet for the first time in her life. After several arguments they eventually kicked Joann out of the house. Jean woke up one morning and her sister and protector was gone. Joann took a job at a grocery store in Dayton and later moved in with an aunt when the father of her baby took off.

In September, Doreen and Alonzo reluctantly used their indoor toilet money for the remainder of the tuition that wasn't covered by Jean's scholarship and she was told to pack up. She threw what little she had into a bag and walked down to the small bus station alone. She bought a ticket and boarded the bus to Yellow Springs. No one came to the station to see her off or wish her luck. Terrified, her hands shook and she clenched them in her lap as the bus started down the dirt road out of town. Now that her twin was gone there was nothing left for her at home. She planned on never returning.

★ ★ ★

YELLOW Springs, Ohio, was a liberal town on the banks of the Ohio River, with a long history of racial tolerance. Antioch College was its bastion for like-minded young people. It was just down Interstate 68 from Jean's hometown, but a world away. The colorful main street was filled with hippie coffee shops and secondhand clothing stores. The hundred-acre campus was within walking distance of downtown, spread out over rolling hills of old-stand trees and red-brick Georgian architecture. College was everything this articulate, rural girl had dreamed of. Jean had a cramped and dirty dorm room all to herself, which seemed positively decadent after the crowded and raucous confines of the farm. For the first couple of weeks the culture shock was profound and dizzying.

Jean walked around with her head down and stuck to what she knew best: studying. But beyond her room, the campus scene was blazing with the turbulent civil rights and women's movements. The Vietnam War was raging overseas, and the Kent State shootings—where the Ohio National Guard shot and killed four students who were protesting the war—had happened the year before just up the I-95. One night, Jean attended a feminist civil rights meeting that was being held at her dorm and was taken by the passion of the women participants. She marveled at the ease with which these Black and brown women carried themselves and spoke up. The way they assumed the world would have to bend to them instead of the other way around. Jean was shocked; she had never been taught that her opinion as a young Black girl mattered. Now, suddenly, she began to tap into her Black identity, and she eagerly became more politically involved, throwing herself into the counterculture scene.

In her second semester she marched in anti-war protests against America's involvement in Vietnam, attended feminist art lectures, and grooved to Thelonious Monk concerts under the stars. Jean had always felt like an outsider in her hometown and even with her family, but here she quickly found her people. She had never had a group of friends before, but she began to hang out with a multicultural mix of female intellectuals and civil rights radicals. Jean decided to change her name to DuShaun because she thought it sounded French, grew out her Afro and took a liking to African-print dashikis that she found in the vintage shops. Her grades began to suffer, but for once she didn't care. She spent hours talking politics on the school's wide front lawn that rolled away toward the Ohio River, her new life suddenly filled with passion and possibilities. Then, one night, DuShaun woke with intense, searing cramps. They came in crashing waves that rendered her breathless and afraid for her life. She barely got dressed and a friend rushed her to the emergency room. She moaned in agony as she grasped the hospital bed rails, but the doctors couldn't find anything wrong with her. Eventually, mercifully, the pain subsided and she was sent home. The next morning, Joann called and told her twin that she had given birth to a baby girl the night before. She realized it had been her sister's pain she had felt. Although DuShaun loved her twin, she was now more certain than ever that she would never be like her.

★ ★ ★

ONE evening after class near the end of her first year at Antioch, as she was strolling across the courtyard, DuShaun stopped to watch an outdoor student play. The only white boy in the production was a skinny Jewish kid in the role of a princely frog, leaping around the stage. The play was based on an African fairy tale about a Black queen who falls prey to the love of a charming frog in a princely disguise. DuShaun was drawn to the actor's wild, free spirit and, feeling confident, decided to introduce herself.

Chapter Three

THE FROG PRINCE'S NAME WAS STANLEY GRANOFSKY, and he was also fumbling his way through his first year. He had come to Antioch from Toronto, Canada, in the hopes of finding himself. He spent his first semester in Ohio wandering around with a map, feeling lost and alone. But after a few weeks he'd slowly become immersed in the theater program and was beginning to thrive. He had been raised in a wealthy, conservative Jewish family and had felt at odds with his upbringing for most of his life. The year before, when a friend told him he was going down to school at Antioch in Ohio, Stanley had applied on a whim and been accepted. Intending to study theater, literature and photography, he thought that the school's culture might suit him. His parents, Phil and Shirley Granofsky, hoped it would give him some direction.

The Granofskys were descended from Jews who'd fled the Russian pogroms in the early 1900s. Stanley's paternal grandparents, Abraham and Pearl Granofsky, left in 1920 after an aunt was murdered on her doorstep by the Bolsheviks. Abraham had been an ambitious entrepreneur and had had a successful soap-manufacturing business in Minsk. But he was betrayed by a non-Jewish partner and sold out to the Communists. The business was seized, leaving their growing family penniless.

Pregnant and weary, they crossed the border into Romania by bribing a guard. Several hard years later, they traveled by ship with their two children, Phil and Sia, and arrived in Halifax, Canada, in January of 1927. Everything of value they owned had been sewn into hidden pockets in their threadbare coats. They made their way to Toronto, where they had an uncle and aunt who had agreed to put them up. The family quickly settled into an area known as "the Ward."

The Ward was Canada's most notorious neighborhood in the early 1900s, an urban, multicultural Wild West morality tale told in vivid, riotous detail. As the clouds of the Second World War were gathering, the Ward entered its most famous and fertile period. It may have been Canada's biggest and most famous slum, but it was also the center of cultural and immigrant life in the country. The descendants of Black refugees from slavery, Jews fleeing the revolutions in Eastern Europe, Irish, Italian and

Chinese—all made their home in the Ward. Gambling dens and bootlegging operations flourished alongside churches and shmata factories.

Some of the first settlers of the Ward in the early 1900s were descendants of Black American refugees from slavery. Their ancestors' arduous journey to freedom had brought them to spots along the US-Canadian border such as Amherstburg and Essex County. Places like this had become terminal stations for the secret routes, networks and safe houses that made up the Underground Railroad. Many settled in the surrounding countryside, and their children and grandchildren made their way to Toronto and eventually the Ward. There they founded a strong, vibrant community centered around the churches. Many generations of these men and women called the Ward home, and in this setting—five downtown blocks in the center of the city—several Black families grew prosperous and powerful.

Chinese restaurants were ubiquitous along Elizabeth Street, one of the Ward's main thoroughfares. It was a place to work and a landing community for Chinese immigrants to Canada. These restaurants became famous for their food, late-night bacchanals and backroom gambling dens. Canadians from across the country would come to Elizabeth Street to gamble and drink. The restaurants' dining rooms were used by politicians and business tycoons for off-the-record meetings and backroom deals.

Jewish immigrants who, like my father's family, were fleeing the violence raging in Europe, flowed into the Ward en masse in the early 1910s. The striving Jewish community set up businesses and built synagogues and Yiddish Lyric theaters. Jewish grandmothers, Bubbys, were known to be the most fearsome and famous bootleggers during Prohibition. Many young Jewish people worked in the burgeoning shmata and haberdashery factories, the most famous of which was the Eaton Company.

The T. Eaton Company towered over the Ward, symbolically and physically. Its massive brick buildings surrounded the neighborhood and housed the largest factory in Canada. Nine thousand people worked in the Eaton factories, making them the third-largest employer in the country. They employed a Ford Motor production model, where products were sent along a conveyor belt in pieces and put together at stations along the route, and were the first in Canada to sell their merchandise through a mail-order catalog. Many of the Ward's young people worked in the factory sewing clothing and making goods for shipment across the country. This made the Eaton Company incredibly influential in the Ward's politics and pocketbook. Around this time, the young, mostly Jewish tailors and seamstresses began organizing to protest the low salaries and dangerous working conditions at the factories. Sir John Eaton, chief executive officer of Eatons and a scion of the Canadian establishment, viciously fought back, going to battle with his employees. This set off an incendiary civil war that threatened to engulf the company and the neighborhood. After mass protests where thousands of workers and their allies filled the streets, the strike was ultimately unsuccessful. The union failed and the workers filed back to the sewing floors and conveyor belts. But their protests stirred up a culture of activism in the Ward and a virulent anti-Semitism in the surrounding city. This was the world my grandfather's family faced as they settled in two rented rooms in the Jewish Quarter of downtown Toronto in 1927.

* * *

My grandfather, Phil Granofsky, grew up on those rough and tumble streets where the anti-Semitism was rampant, pervasive and violent. In the summer of 1933, when Phil was in his early teens, a championship baseball game took place in Christie Pits, a former quarry turned park in downtown Toronto's west side. The Pits, as it was called, was known to be unsafe and treacherous after dark. But it was a bright, sunny afternoon, and Phil was the mascot for the Jewish boys baseball team that was playing against St. Peter's, a team of Catholic boys. The Jews and Catholics were sworn enemies and tensions were running high. Some of the St. Peter's spectators came armed with chains and iron bars, and when they unveiled a large swastika at the end of the game, a fight broke out.

With the Jewish boys outnumbered, trucks were dispatched into the heart of the Jewish neighborhoods to bring back well-known fighters. The trucks returned, driving in fast with young pugilists hanging off of the running boards, men filled with an explosive, pent-up rage. When the fighting began my grandfather scrambled up a tree. As the fighting became more vicious, he stayed hidden for hours, terrified. Police on horseback eventually arrived, but they remained at the top of the park watching the violence. Smirks on their faces, hands casually on hips. Enjoying the spectacle. Letting them kill each other.

* * *

PHIL's father, Abe, was still an inveterate entrepreneur, and he had already tried a candle-making endeavor in his new country. That failed, but by the 1940s, he had started and was running a grocery importing business and had moved the family to Kensington Market.

Kensington Market became a market in the early 1900s, and Jewish immigrants like my grandfather's family, who had originally settled in the Ward, began to move into the area and set up shops that served other Jews. Stalls were built in front of homes and wares were displayed on the sidewalk, much like in the shtetls many had left behind in the old country. Vendors sold live chickens, ducks and fish, pickles and pickled herring in wooden barrels. Kensington had more than thirty synagogues, one on almost every corner. The neighborhood was a rare and welcome respite from the anti-Semitism and discrimination that darkened their daily lives outside of those few vibrant blocks.

It was here that Abe and his family ran their grocery business importing items such as walnuts, filberts, buckwheat and herring. The fish was brought in from Newfoundland and Iceland. Nuts were brought in from Madagascar, and tea in bulk from Ceylon. Phil's mother, Pearl, worked in the kitchen, loading and unloading deliveries of produce and dry goods. Phil and his boyhood friends worked with Abe on delivery and money collection. Their cousin Elsie, a bookkeeper, set up at the kitchen table, where she would keep the accounts and package products. Family friends worked in the basement bottling oil, and a neighbor drove the delivery truck. The kitchen was often full of men from the neighborhood bartering, kvetching and filling orders. As family lore tells it, one day a Victor Adding Machine salesman arrived at the door to demonstrate the value of adding machines to a growing business. He read out a row of figures, five down and five across. Because of the slow speed at which the drums of the machine worked, Phil had the correct answer before the adding machine did, to the amazement of the salesman and the men gathered around the table. It turned out Phil was something of a math prodigy and after that, he was often called on to settle financial disputes between the older grocers.

At this time, the war raged on in Europe, and young Jewish men from the neighborhood were signing up with great fanfare to fight for Canada. Phil tried to enlist but was turned away after his physical. Sickly all his life, he had had rheumatic fever as a young child in Romania and it had led to undetected heart and valve problems known as rheumatic heart disease. He had also been born with multiple epiphyseal dysplasia, a genetic hip displacement that caused him to limp. The condition would bedevil him his entire life and had already stunted his growth. After being turned away from the military, Phil threw himself into the family business.

The war boom was on and the import business earned a good living for the Granofsky family, but the work was backbreaking. In the winter of 1946, Abe was beginning to have health problems of his own, and Phil realized his father was not going to be able to keep up his relentless work ethic. With his father aging rapidly and his own ongoing hip issues, they were going to have to figure out a less arduous way of making money. At the time, the business was looking for a cheaper way to package their products. They were currently using wooden crates for deliveries, but the crates would often go missing and were too expensive. So, against Abe's better judgment, Phil convinced his father to invest in a machine to make a brand-new packaging product: paper bags. They cobbled their entire savings together, purchased the machine and set it up in their back shed, where it had a chicken coop and a kosher wine distillery as neighbors. Shit and Shinola. Boards formed a path leading from the house to the shed that sunk in the mud when it rained. Abe and Phil spent long hours experimenting on a prototype, with Pearl bringing their dinner to the shed. Eventually, they figured out how to make a low-priced, durable paper bag, and they established Atlantic Paper Products.

In the beginning, they went door-to-door selling Atlantic paper bags to the Jewish businesses in Kensington Market. They had figured out that no matter the business, everyone needed bags to carry their products. Business by business, Phil worked his confident charm and persuasiveness to convince owners to buy from Atlantic. Atlantic Paper Products quickly established itself in the community and began to turn a tidy profit. That same year, on a rare break from work, Phil was on vacation at a Jewish singles resort for young people. There he met and quickly married my grandmother, Shirley Rockfeld.

★ ★ ★

THE Rockfelds, Shirley's family, were already well established in the Ward when Phil arrived with his family in the late 1920s. Three generations of Rockfelds lived under one roof, and they thrived in a tight-knit community. On Friday, Shirley would arrive home from school to the aroma of the Shabbat meal mingling with the clean scent of wax and polish. Her mother and aunts would have spent the day down on their hands and knees scrubbing the floor, gossiping and admonishing each other. Shirley's grandmother, Malka, would have cooked on a wood-burning stove in the kitchen to make challahs, yeast doughs, honey cake and kichlach. The gefilte fish would have been chopped by hand with a cleaver and, more often than not, that fish was so fresh it had been swimming in the bathtub just hours before.

Aaron and Malka Shimmerman, Shirley's grandparents, had immigrated to Canada in the early 1900s. Aaron came from Poland and sent for his family after he had established himself. Malka made the perilous trip by boat alone with their six children, sick and breastfeeding their youngest. They settled in a shack in the Ward where Shirley was born, but eventually made enough money to buy a house where their children and grandchildren could all live together. Aaron had been married once before in the old country, and while his first wife had died in childbirth, a daughter named Tsivia had survived. When Aaron and Malka left Poland, Tsivia had begged to go with them, but Malka had left her behind with her mother's family. Tsivia continued to write to them in Canada, pleading with them to send for her. Malka refused, claiming she had enough children to look after. Eventually, Tsivia made it over on her own, marrying a baker from Toronto who was divorced with two daughters. Shirley grew up with the two girls, Lillian and Gertrude, as cousins, and spent many hours playing at their house.

Tsivia's new Canadian husband, the baker, was Harry Tobin, a meek man who kept to himself after Tsivia took over the household. The girls' mother was the infamous Bessie Starkman, the notorious female mob boss. Bessie had been a fairly conventional housewife when she was young, but she had been desperately unhappy in her marriage to Harry and found her role as a mother boring and unfulfilling. In 1912, the Tobins were renting out rooms in their house on Chestnut Street to boarders for extra money. Rocco Perri, a dashing and brash young immigrant from the Calabria region of Italy, rented one. Within a year, Bessie had abandoned her husband and daughters to join Rocco in Hamilton, Ontario, where she lived as his common-law wife.

Hamilton was an up-and-coming hardscrabble steel town southwest of Toronto along the shore of Lake Ontario, close to the American border. At the time, Hamilton was rife with corruption and crime, and powerful steel magnates built fortunes out of its scorched earth. The city was a complicated mix of wealth and lawlessness and it was there, together, that Bessie and Rocco built a multimillion-dollar bootlegging business after the Ontario Temperance Act (OTA) became law. The OTA was the government's doomed and stunningly misguided attempt to wrest power from organized crime by prohibiting the sale of alcohol before US Prohibition. Predictably, Hamilton's convenient location made it particularly attractive to mobsters who imported alcohol from the United States. While Rocco was the corpulent, bombastic face of the organization, Bessie controlled the behind-the-scenes business and negotiations. It was Bessie who placed the orders with the distilleries and breweries, laundered the money and handled the bank accounts. She quickly rose to become underboss of the Perri organized crime family by being audacious, arrogant, violent and organized. She was the first woman to rise so publicly in an organized crime family. Known to dress extravagantly, she draped herself in furs, jewelry and silks, cutting an elegant figure in a rough, blue-collar town. She was also a guilt-ridden and regretful mother, inquiring about her girls often and sending for them when Tsivia would allow it.

My grandmother would often be at her cousins' home when large ribboned boxes would arrive from Hamilton for Lillian and Gertrude. Inside were beautiful dresses made of lace and silk with matching stoles and gloves that the girls would delight in. Tsivia, a vengeful and controlling stepmother, would then gather the clothing and burn it in front of the three girls, jealously preaching temperance under the enviable guise of morality. She maintained a simmering resentment toward Bessie, and when Shirley would visit, she refused to have the woman's name spoken in their home. It went on like this until August 13, 1930, when Bessie was killed by a single shotgun blast as she and Rocco were leaving their modest split-level home. Her body riddled with holes, her corpse was photographed and splashed across the front page of national newspapers. Thousands attended her funeral, breaking through police lines at the small Jewish cemetery south of Hamilton, toppling fences and trampling gravestones. Rocco collapsed at his lover's graveside, weeping and rending his clothing. His open display of grief making his square-jawed bodyguards avert their eyes in embarrassment. It was the biggest funeral in Hamilton's history. The girls were not allowed to attend and never spoke of it.

* * *

As a teenager, Shirley's favorite evening activity was attending the Saturday show at the local theater with her mother, Toby. The Royal theater, built in 1939, was an art deco jewel box that delighted the teenager. With the purchase of a ticket, each moviegoer was also given a dinner plate or a cup and saucer: delphine bone china, gilt-edged and hand-painted with delicate pale flowers, and *Made in England* stamped on the bottom. This practice allowed many residents of the neighborhood without means to accumulate a complete set of dinnerware—and came with the added convenience of being able to borrow your neighbors' matching set if you were hosting guests. The showings of *The Wizard of Oz* and *Gone with the Wind* were paired with particularly popular patterns. Inevitably, during a crucial moment in the film, someone would drop a dish and the entire crowd would laugh.

Despite Shirley's trips to the movies, money for extras was generally slim. At home, everything was used and recycled; nothing could ever go to waste. Sugar sacks were saved and made into dishtowels, aprons and pillowcases. For years, the family slept on scratchy, burlap pillows with lettering that read *granulated sugar*. Toilet paper was another luxury the family could not afford. Instead, they used the tissue paper that came wrapped around individual oranges in the crate. Toby would smooth out the tissue and hang it on a nail in the bathroom wall. During the hard winter months, the entire family of eight shared a bed next to the boiler, switching positions throughout the night so everyone had a shift closest to the heat. There were hardships, to be sure, but family, faith and community gave meaning and shape to their lives.

* * *

In the summer of 1946, Shirley and her best friend had saved up all year to attend Smith's Bay House, a summer resort for Jewish singles in Port Carling, Ontario, a picturesque beach town on the shores of Lake Muskoka. For Toronto's young Jewish community, Smith's Bay House was a cottage country respite from the city's sweltering heat. Barred from the gentile resorts, these young men and women flocked to its cabins and beaches. During the day, Shirley swam in the lake and then sat, with her long, pretty legs, sunning herself on a rock at the shore's edge. At night she danced in the dining hall to live music played by the same young men who worked as the resort's waiters during the day. The dining tables were pushed to the side and lights hung from the rafters in strings. It led to magical, sweaty nights and chaotic breakfast services. There, she met Phil and they quickly fell in love, marrying within the year after a whirlwind romance. Once she was married, Shirley moved out of her grandparents' house and in with Phil's parents and siblings in their crowded Kensington Market home. Phil was beginning to build the newly renamed Atlantic Packaging Products up from the one-machine operation in his family's back shed into a company worth hundreds of millions of dollars.

Atlantic had already been well established in the Jewish community and the company was thriving with the help of local businesses. But Phil wanted to break into the wider non-Jewish business community, where opportunities were far more lucrative. He used his Jewish business connections, several of whom had non-Jewish clients, and adeptly wrangled introductions. International shipping was growing exponentially in those years and Atlantic Packaging, which had expanded its business from paper bags into cardboard box manufacturing, was perfectly positioned to help these multinational companies ship their products. Phil was charming and incredibly persistent, taking managers out to lunch and donating generously to their bosses' philanthropic projects. This would become a very successful constant in Phil's life, combining business with charitable giving. By the time Stanley, their third child, was born in 1952, business was on a tear. Shirley had had a traumatic birth experience with Stanley. Her doctor had not been available when she went into labor, so he ordered the nurses to keep her legs crossed until he could arrive. Writhing in agony, she had begged them to let her push. The doctor did finally arrive in a tuxedo, slightly perturbed at the inconvenience, having been at a black tie affair. The emotional scars of that traumatic birth would linger through her fourth and final pregnancy and the birth of their last child a couple of years later.

Moving up in the world along with the company, Shirley and Phil bought a duplex on Bathurst Street, a main thoroughfare in another Jewish neighborhood that was more of a striving and modern middle-class spot compared to Kensington Market, with its old country roots. Several of the kids' friends in the neighborhood were the children of Holocaust survivors. Their friends' parents would smoke cigarettes and cry silently as they listened to "Exodus" played on the piano after dinner. A vast and shattered sadness lurked behind a frenetic new immigrant productivity. Several years later, with Atlantic expanding to two factory plants in the north end of the city, Phil and Shirley built their dream house in the upscale Bridle Path neighborhood.

The Bridle Path was a verdant and luxurious new neighborhood in Toronto's north end. Because the homes and money were new, the anti-Semitism prevalent in other wealthy and more established "old money" neighborhoods was not as much of a factor here. Huge mansions with turrets were being built on wide, rolling lots with grand driveways. The Granofsky house was a classic red-brick colonial sprawl with white Grecian pillars, a swimming pool, tennis court and rolling green gardens—the same house I would one day visit. Phil and Shirley moved their four children in and began hosting fundraisers and business dinners. Shirley was a brilliant and astute social partner to Phil's business acumen. He would call her after work and tell her he was bringing home potential clients, and she would have a multi-course dinner plated and her hair and makeup done by the time they rolled up the driveway. Together, they always landed the deal.

As they became more prosperous, they established themselves as pillars of the Jewish community, eventually donating millions of dollars to charities like the United Jewish Appeal. Phil sat on the boards of international Jewish charities and became a central player in Israeli politics and fundraising. They had built the life of their dreams, and for an ambitious immigrant family, appearances were everything. The children, especially the boys, were expected to fall in line and follow their father into business.

★ ★ ★

My father, Stanley, had a privileged childhood growing up in that family and going to a solidly middle-class Hebrew day school. He had a good group of friends who all lived in his neighborhood, and he spent his weekends riding bikes or swimming in someone's backyard pool. In the summer, Stanley attended a Jewish fine arts camp, where he first fell in love with theater. Camp Manitouwabing sat on its namesake lake several hours north of Toronto. It was an arts-focused camp that offered acting, music and painting, as well as sailing, waterskiing and archery. One afternoon, Stanley hit five bull's-eyes in a row and was known from then on as one of the best shots in camp, an honorific he carried proudly through grade school.

At school, he was a smart kid who by the second grade had been pulled out of the regular courses and put in an accelerated class. It was a streamed program, which eventually meant the children graduated from high school in four years rather than the five years typical in the Ontario curriculum at the time. The program was competitive and challenging, and Stanley excelled in it. But it also meant he graduated a year before his cohort and would be the youngest in his class when he attended Antioch. That age gap caused a gnawing insecurity that would plague him through his years in high school and college. It was a volatile combination of high intelligence and immaturity.

★ ★ ★

AT home, Stanley was starting to resent Phil's coldness as a father and his relentless drive to achieve. Phil was a wonderfully charming businessman and a loving husband, but he was a completely absent father. He was absorbed in his own ambitions, community work and political connections. He worked brutally long hours, and when he was home he showed little interest in his children. He was also often sick and in pain from his many physical ailments, which led to multiple heart and hip operations. He would convalesce at home and the kids were expected to make themselves scarce. His father's inability to show affection for his children, and particularly his sons, wounded Stanley deeply.

It was the late sixties, and as a teenager, Stanley was desperate to shed the burden of his parent's old-school expectations. He grew his hair long, wore hip-hugging corduroy bell-bottoms and smoked pot while listening to Miles Davis. He switched high schools in the eleventh grade and made new friends who also listened to jazz and the blues and had little regard for their parents' generation. His grades began to suffer, and the conflicts with his parents, especially Phil, became more acrimonious. "You don't give a shit about me, man! You think you can tell me what to do, come in and play the authoritarian." He was a long-haired, angry iconoclast, and his parents couldn't relate to him at all.

Due to his accelerated classes early in school, Stanley was only seventeen in his last year of high school, and already chafing at the bit. Every day after school he would walk home and his path took him along the back of a large horse farm famous for housing Canada's most decorated racehorse in his old age. Northern Dancer had gained international fame in 1964 when he won the Kentucky Derby, the Preakness Stakes and the Queen's Plate all in the same year. The famous retired horse was often out in the field when Stanley walked by after school, and it would sometimes walk alongside him. Stanley began to bring carrots and apples to feed him and would pet the animal as it ate. A lost, angry boy and a champion past his prime.

That year, a friend from his years at Manitouwabing told him about the college he was attending in the United States, a place Stanley had never heard of called Antioch College in Yellow Springs, Ohio. Stanley checked it out and applied at the last minute when his parents threatened to make him get a job if he didn't find somewhere to go after high school. He was accepted into the theater program and found that the school's radical culture appealed to him. His parents weren't thrilled with the theater major but were just happy he had some kind of direction.

Chapter Four

STANLEY FLEW DOWN TO OHIO THE SUMMER BEFORE his freshmen year to get settled in his dorm and explore the campus. Alone except for his buddy, who was in another program, he kept a creased map in his back pocket and spent most of his time feeling lost. Eventually classes started, and Stanley was immediately taken with the courses. The subjects were dynamic and taught by world-famous teachers. Cecil Taylor, a pianist and renowned musical radical, was teaching in the music program at the time. Stanley fell in with the theater crowd, and his professor would have the students over for dinner and conversation at his arts and crafts–style house. Stanley began to thrive in his theater classes, landing the lead role in a one-act play by Eugene O'Neill. His feelings of insecurity had slowly begun to abate and, on a lark, he joined a couple of other theater students who were putting on an African play.

* * *

DuSHAUN stopped and watched the play, joining other students who were sitting on the grass, the sun slanting across Antioch's courtyard. On the makeshift stage Stanley was wild and hilarious, completely committed and vulnerable. She felt an instant connection to the skinny young man, recognizing in him her own awkward yearning to be free. As the play wrapped up, people applauded and quietly dispersed. Only DuShaun lingered, trying to appear occupied and nonchalant. As Stanley left the stage, she shyly introduced herself, telling him how much she enjoyed his performance. They fell into an easy conversation, and he invited her to the after-party at his dorm room. They walked toward his residence together, unhurried as the sun set and twilight descended across campus. They spent the evening sitting on his unmade mattress on the floor, drinking mulled wine and discussing politics, race and religion. My mother had never knowingly met a Jewish person before, and my father had never really talked with a Black woman in his life. They were mysteries to each other. Their worlds were so diametrically opposed. He could know nothing of her life on the farm and growing up poor and Black in rural Ohio. The hole in the wall that was a room of her own, the whippings she bore and her fight to be free of it all. She could know nothing of his life on the Bridle Path in a city in Canada where he grew up wealthy and Jewish. The pressure brought to bear on him by a disapproving father and the opulent, stifling home that he was running from. They only knew that they wanted to be near each other. And after that evening, they fell into a passionate on-again, off-again relationship.

* * *

It was 1972, a time of great turmoil and hope on dusty back roads and in shining lecture halls. Campus protests against the Vietnam War ended in violence with state troopers. In Ohio, the women's movement and the civil rights movement were being met with a virulent conservative backlash. Stanley and DuShaun had deep, impassioned political conversations in the colorful coffee shops that lined the main road of Yellow Springs. She liked that he was educated and funny, and that he listened to her. She had never been heard like that before, his thoughtful listening like a revelation. He thought she was sexy, assertive and direct. He liked that she had an intellectual fervor and plans to get as far away from her upbringing as she could. Stanley hadn't spoken to his parents in months and was feeling untethered from his home life. Adrift. For the two of them, lying hot in his messy dorm room, the expanse of their skin, so pale white and deep brown, felt radical in its very opposition.

From childhood, DuShaun had lived with the reality of a blood condition that would likely prevent her from having children. Her periods had always been erratic and unpredictable, and she was constantly having nosebleeds. As a result of her childhood diagnosis, she and Stanley thought they didn't have to use protection. He was assured it was impossible for her to become pregnant and was happy enough to believe it. It was not unusual for her to miss several periods, so she wasn't concerned until she started to feel nauseous. She took a pregnancy test and sat on the toilet shocked—she was pregnant. To my mother, it was a miracle pregnancy. Something she'd never thought would happen to her. To my father, it was cataclysmic news. He was utterly unprepared to be a father, financially dependent on his parents and still battling a lingering sense of insecurity and angst. He was into DuShaun, but she was just a girl he was dating and he definitely wasn't looking for a commitment. He felt trapped and lied to. In a panic, my father asked her to have an abortion. She refused, delighted with the news that she was going to be a mom. She was sure that she could avoid the fate of her sister, Joann, who now had two daughters by two different absent men and worked a dead-end job. DuShaun believed she could make a pregnancy, her schooling and this relationship work. She was twenty-two; Stanley had just turned nineteen.

That winter they drove to Toronto to break the news of the pregnancy to Stanley's parents, who knew nothing of the relationship. For DuShaun, the trip was into two unknowns: an unsuspecting family in a mysterious country. There had been a map on the wall in DuShaun's grade-school classroom; the area above the United States was just a blank space with one word—*Canada*. No lines or borders or lakes or cities. No provinces, territories or capital cities. For years, she thought Canada was the name of the map company.

They had left Ohio that morning and driven straight up to Toronto listening to Joni Mitchell as an introduction to the country. They borrowed an old beater from a friend that had a sticky second gear that you had to grind into place and which gave Stanley trouble the whole drive. He wore his Che Guevara T-shirt and ripped bell-bottoms. A few months earlier he had let his hair grow out and was now attempting a patchy beard. My mother was in her best African-print wrap-dress, a Black Power button proudly fastened to her coat. As they pulled up the driveway, she realized that her elbows were ashy and desperately dug in her fringed bag for lotion. Stanley let the engine die a slow, guttural death as they parked in the glow of the mansion's decorative lights. Deep silence. The kind of silence you can only get on a winter's night or in the pause after the words *I don't love you anymore*. Stanley was trying to steel himself but was sick with nerves. Shocked, DuShaun took in the size of the house. She knew Stanley's family was well-off but it hadn't even occurred to her that he was rich. Like rich

rich. Her heart began to hammer, a bird trying to escape its cage. "It's huge. Why didn't you tell me?" Stanley could only shrug his shoulders. "I didn't think you'd ever be here." She craned her neck to see up to the roof and along the rows of shuttered windows, looking out over the vast property with a growing unease.

She realized this was something altogether different than she had imagined. It wasn't just a visit, it was an ambush. DuShaun took a deep breath and tried to steady herself. "It's going to be alright, Stanley. Just give it a chance." He shook his head. "You don't understand. They're going to freak out." DuShaun turned to face him. "This baby is good news. For Jews, a baby is a blessing. I was looking it up the other day." He shook his head. "You have no idea."

Without another word Stanley exited the van, door squeaking. DuShaun, still feeling slightly optimistic in the face of the shitstorm she now knew she was about to enter, stepped out too, their deep, shaky breath turning into plumes of crystallized air.

* * *

THEY rang the doorbell at the massive front entrance and waited. DuShaun noticed the mezuzah on the doorframe. Having never seen one, she reached out and touched it gently, wondering at the carved vines and flowers in the cold silver. Stanley grimaced slightly and shook his head and she quickly drew her hand away. They heard Shirley's heels in the foyer and then the large front doors opened. Shirley had been expecting her son for a visit and greeted him with a smile. When she caught sight of DuShaun standing next to him she was surprised. Her face registered shock and then an uncertain dread settled in. What could this be about? She could read her son's nervous slouch and could tell something was wrong. DuShaun realized that Stanley hadn't told his parents that she was even coming, and she cursed him silently. The two women looked at Stanley, and Stanley, wishing he was anywhere but there, looked at the ground. Shirley greeted DuShaun reservedly and, realizing she couldn't keep them standing at the front door, stood aside and let them in.

The evening didn't go well.

* * *

SHIRLEY had gathered Phil, and the four of them now stood in the kitchen, drinking coffee while Stanley awkwardly introduced them. Shirley politely mentioned that she had recently read a copy of *Essence* and that she and Phil had both supported the Freedom Riders back in the sixties. Phil had just arrived home from work and was still wearing a three-piece suit. He was short in stature but intimidating when he wanted to be. He stood staring at his son and glancing briefly at DuShaun as she and Shirley made stiff small talk. Eventually the room fell silent and it became obvious that something needed to be said. Stanley dove in, meeting his father's gaze. "DuShaun and I have been . . . hanging out. For about a year. She told me she couldn't get pregnant and I believed her. And now we're having a baby and you're just going to have to deal with it."

It took a moment for Phil and Shirley to realize that their son was trying to tell them their first grandchild was going to be a half-Black, non-Jewish American Methodist born to a woman they hadn't known more than twenty minutes. There was an excruciating silence as the reality of what was being said sank in. Then Phil immediately accused DuShaun, an older woman, of bamboozling their naive son into fathering a child and looking for a payout. My grandfather stood up and started shouting, "I'm not supporting this child or this woman!" My father turned on him. "I'm not looking for your handouts, you fascist!" Phil was enraged and astounded. "Fool. How could you be such a fool!" The two descended into a screaming match. Phil repeated his threat to financially cut his son off if he chose to do this. Shirley paced, clutching her pearls.

DuShaun stood silently, cemented to the spot, coffee cup still in her hand. How could she have been so stupid, thinking this child would have been welcomed? Now she just wanted to disappear, and prayed her stillness might somehow make her invisible. When all the vile, hateful recriminations had been shouted and repeated, Stanley grabbed DuShaun's hand and stormed out of the house. Tumbling back into the bleak winter, the cold a shocking, welcome reprieve from the hellfire situation they were fleeing. They got into the van and slammed the squeaking doors behind them. My father started the engine but then sat unmoving. He trembled, terrified for his future. My mother cried bitterly, humiliated and wondering for the first time how they would make ends meet. The suddenly bleak prospect of zero support from either of their families settled in, the social and cultural issues they were about to face just now beginning to make themselves clear. Finally, Stanley ground the gear into place and they drove back into the night.

★ ★ ★

AFTER several heated phone calls, Phil made good on his threat and cut his son off financially. They were heartbroken that their first grandchild was not going to be Jewish and felt cheated and scammed. This was Stanley's mess and he'd have to figure out a way to support this family on his own. For several months Stanley and DuShaun continued in school, moving into his tiny dorm room together to save money. It was immediately clear that they were not well suited for the struggle ahead. Stanley was still angry about a niggling, unspoken belief that he had been lied to and tricked into the situation. This was only enflamed and encouraged by his parents' continuing accusations. DuShaun was furious that she was being suspected of something so nefarious. Her joy at being able to conceive retreated into a defensive crouch. It also became harder for her to concentrate in class. She was having a very difficult pregnancy, sick and unable to hold any food down. With her condition, the risk of miscarriage was high and her blood pressure had to be monitored constantly. Stanley still wanted to go out, be a kid and participate in college life. They began to fight. Eventually my mother had to go on bed rest and Stanley's tuition fees went unpaid and then they had no choice.

He and my mother dropped out of school. With nowhere else to go, they went back to her family farm. The farm was still crowded with siblings, nieces, nephews and cousins. Doreen and Alonzo still slept on the bed in the living room, and the two upstairs bedrooms had long been claimed by older siblings with their own families. Her father shook his head, looking the two bedraggled castoffs up and down. "Uh-uh, we don't need no more people up on that second floor. Jeanie, you're going to have to make room some other way."

DuShaun and Stanley were eventually given a mattress on the screened-in porch and made their home there. "You're gonna get hot as Hades out here around noon but it oughta cool down for you in the night." DuShaun hung tie-dye scarves up for curtains to try to give them privacy from the constant coming and going in the morning. At night it did cool down and the sounds of the farm grew quiet with the relief of the setting sun. Neither one of them had experience getting a job, and my father wasn't legally allowed to work in the States anyway. Unmoored, he started doing yoga to get centered and helped out around the farm where he could. By this time the farm wasn't a working farm anymore, the animals long sold off and the garden growing a bit wild as the kids grew up and spread out and Doreen and Alonzo got older. But there was always something to do or mend or fix. Stanley was an object of amusement and curiosity to DuShaun's family—a white, Canadian Jewish kid with long hair and raggedy clothes who didn't know the first thing about farming. My father wasn't built for hard labor but he tried to be of use, digging ditches and mending fences. He and my mother's siblings and cousins would work out in the fields, stopping under the sweltering sun for lunch and lemonade that my mother, feeling slightly better in her last trimester, would dutifully bring out. Her belly full and her hips widening. My father, pink and sweating profusely, enjoyed the working-man camaraderie and took her brothers' muscular ribbing easily. But inside, he was lost and growing increasingly desperate to find some way out of this situation. He especially hated watching DuShaun's siblings and their own children. Almost all of the brothers and sisters still lived within driving distance of where they were raised, and they spent the weekends hanging out at each other's homes. Joann had also moved back after the birth of her second daughter and lived down the road. Stanley would watch in shock as some of the siblings would beat their children and yell at them mercilessly for small, typically childish mistakes. They would often get the "switch" and whip the kids in the middle of a gathering. He couldn't stomach watching it but felt he had no right to step in.

As the weeks passed, he became more and more anxious, and he yearned for meaning and to travel. DuShaun was embarrassed and gutted that she had come crawling back to her family, unmarried, pregnant and a college dropout. Her grand dreams and belief that she was meant for something bigger had come crashing down around her. But as much as they tried, she would not bend to her older, more religious siblings' entreaties to find God and Jesus. Her older sisters would shake their heads at her blasphemy and atheism, though she knew they were secretly thrilled that she was down so low. DuShaun was now living with and dependent on the family she had been running so desperately away from just a couple of years ago. Stanley and DuShaun slept back-to-back on that mattress on the sweltering screened-in porch, tie-dye curtains hanging still in the evening heat. Both churning with unanswerable, terrifying questions. In the mornings, my conservative Black grandfather would look out the window and see my long-haired father doing sun salutations in the back forty. "Jeanie! Your white boy's gettin' naked again!" Pregnant and unemployed, my mother tried to keep the peace.

Around this same time my dad began to follow a spiritual leader named Bhagwan Shree Rajneesh. Bhagwan had built a small ashram in Bombay—now Mumbai—India, where he introduced the practice of "dynamic meditation," a mix of Hinduism and psychotherapy that, according to Bhagwan, enabled people to experience divinity. Followers from all over the world were making the pilgrimage to the ashram to hear Bhagwan speak. Several of Stanley's old buddies from Toronto were traveling over and told him he should do the same. After a sleepless night, my father decided he had to meet this guru. It felt as if he was being drawn to something important and escaping at the same time.

He told my mother his decision while sitting on their mattress eating oatmeal the next morning. "I'll be back in time for the birth. I promise. I'm not leaving you, I just have to go. Trust me on this, please." My mother became grasping and nervous, scared of being broke, heavily pregnant and left behind on the farm. She angrily tried to get him to stay but my father was insistent, assuring her he would come back for the birth. DuShaun was terrified. The only thing right now that separated her from her broke and single sister working at the grocery store, a job for which DuShaun would now be grateful, was this relationship. This belief that she and Stanley could make it through anything and were meant for something better was the last "hail Mary" dream she was hanging on to. When they told her family at dinner that Stanley would be leaving without DuShaun, there was a collective head shake from her siblings. When he assured her parents he would be back for their daughter, her mother just nodded politely. "Mm-hmm." "I knew that white boy wasn't cut out to do the right thing!" Alonzo would admonish his daughter later.

The next morning DuShaun stood at the farm door, anxious and crying, her hand above her eyes to block the sun as Stanley drove away. He had managed to hitch a ride to Dayton with one of my mother's brothers who was visiting a girlfriend there. As he watched the farm recede, he felt the gut punch of the last eight months also fall away. He took a deep, shaky breath and almost laughed out loud, stifling his relief in the presence of family. At the Dayton Municipal Airport, he boarded a plane for the sixteen-hour flight to Bombay. All he was carrying was a small bag with a broken zipper, the last of their money and an inkling that he was chasing his destiny.

Chapter Five

THE SIXTIES AND SEVENTIES WERE A TIME OF GROW-
ing interest, for the Western counterculture movement, in Eastern spiritualism and India. The poet and
radical Malay Roy Choudhury had hosted Allen Ginsberg
for years in Varanasi, and the Beatles had made living on
an ashram hugely popular. By the early seventies, a trickle
had turned into a flood as hippies and nomads from North
America and Europe followed a well-worn trail through
Turkey, Iran, Afghanistan, Pakistan and, finally, India and
Nepal.

It was this scene that Stanley stepped off the plane into.
Bleary-eyed and jet-lagged, he was immediately hit with the
roiling wall of heat, color and smell that was Bombay. He
had arrived at the hottest time of year, and as he descended
to the tarmac he realized the pavement was bubbling. In the

packed terminal he was swept up in the fast-moving stream of humanity flowing toward the doors and the city beyond, eddying near the tuk-tuk stand at the broken sidewalk.

He was quickly cajoled into a vehicle, and the small tuk-tuk careened away from the arrivals terminal. Soon he was flying through the dense slum that surrounded the airport and spilled onto its tarmacs. The driver blared his horn aggressively and swerved around clusters of people, animals and food stalls, the noise and heat and distance conspiring to shock my father into an altered state. Alive. Alive. Alive.

★ ★ ★

BHAGWAN Shree Rajneesh had only recently become an international draw to the hundreds of young Westerners who were now making their way to him. They were attracted by his radical reimagining of sexuality and spirituality and the free-love attitude of his ashram. Like Indian disciples, Western followers like my father now flocked to Rajneesh's presence and teachings. Searching out divinity and a place to stay. To this end, Stanley had written a friend who was already a follower of Bhagwan and living near the ashram. He told him he was coming and asked to stay in his apartment for a few weeks.

He arrived at a small apartment block in a dense neighborhood in the south end of the city to find his friend in the grip of a heroin addiction. The apartment was small and dirty but there was a couch that he could crash on. Bhagwan was speaking later that afternoon in Maidan Park, so his friend welcomed him happily and dug in his closet for red and orange clothes that would fit Stanley. Everyone who came to sit with Bhagwan was asked to wear red, orange, pink or yellow. The colors of the sun. Stanley's friend was much larger than he was, so the clothes were mostly too big for him, but Stanley cinched the belt and rolled up the sleeves. After a quick meal of curry and dhal, they walked to the city center—sweating, cuffs dragging in the dirt, leaving a trail behind him. The crowds began to thicken as they approached the park, and Stanley was picked up in a clamorous, rushing human river. He was completely over-whelmed but buoyed along by his building excitement.

Maidan Park is a huge open field in the heart of Bombay and is the green lungs of the heavily polluted city. A stage had been set up for Bhagwan to address the thousands of worshippers pouring onto the wide garbage-strewn field. As they entered the park, Stanley was lost in the crush of the masses of Indian seekers surging to see the master. Separated from his friend, he began to panic as he was left to navigate the crowd's deluge on his own. But, likely because he was dressed in orange and red and a Westerner, my father was pulled out of the throngs and told to sit up on the stage. Confused, he took a seat at the back of the wide edifice with a large group of strangers who were

77

also wearing the colors of the sun. A single chair was positioned at the front, empty. The air crackled with expectation. When Bhagwan finally emerged, the crowd became hysterical, joyfully dancing, writhing and falling at his feet. He was young and beautiful with wide brown eyes and a long jet-black beard falling against a plain white robe. Even at a distance, he radiated energy, his hands clasped in prayer, smiling beatifically.

Thousands of worshippers stretched into the distance, dancing and singing, the chaotic city in a haze beyond them. My father was, in that moment, exhausted, utterly lost and frantic to be saved. He was a man grasping for hope as everything around him was changing. He had never felt like he belonged in his parents' world and had now been cast out. He had no idea how to be a father to a child he did not want. And he was struggling in a relationship with a woman he was coming to realize he did not love. Feeling as if it was too much to bear, he was swept up in the charged, unadulterated love of the man before him. He wept and fell at the master's feet.

★ ★ ★

WITH a convert's zeal, Stanley fully bought in to being a follower of Bhagwan. Later that week he took Sannyas before his new master. A Sannyasi, in Hinduism, is a religious ascetic who has renounced the world and abandoned

THE GIRL IN THE MIDDLE

all claim to social or family standing. In Sanskrit it means to "abandon" or "throw down." He was given the name Fakeer. A religious beggar. That night, in a laundry sink, he dyed his old clothes red and orange. He began to wear a mala, a necklace with wooden beads, with a black-and-white picture of Bhagwan on it. With his friend's heroin addiction deepening, Stanley moved out of the apartment and into his own room in a shithole hotel downtown called the Rex. The walls didn't go all the way to the ceiling and the bed covers had cigarette burns. His neighbors on the other side of the paper-thin wall were women selling sex to foreigners. In the hotel's shabby lobby there was a fruit juice bar that was a popular hangout for disciples of Bhagwan. Fervid talk of enlightenment mixed with mango pulp, fresh coconut water and whole cracked pepper from Bangladesh. Fakeer sat with his fellow wanderers and reveled in existential discussions deep into the evening. In the morning, Fakeer would stumble out of the Rex, bleary-eyed, into the stifling early heat. Passing the beggars sleeping out front, he would shake one of the taxi drivers awake and ask to be taken to Chowpatty Beach.

The beach was known for its famous nighttime celebrations with snake charmers, food stalls, astrologers and musicians. Fire-eaters would blow flames into the night air as families and groups of teenagers strolled the boardwalk. In the early mornings, though, it was host to a meditation gathering. Fakeer would arrive at the large beach and rush to participate, along with hundreds of worshippers, in a sunrise dynamic meditation. As the sun rose and music played, he would dance wildly and weep openly, throwing energy to the sea. Afterward, he would lie silently on his back in the garbage-strewn sand, exhausted and utterly content as the morning light glittered on the waves, tears pooling in his ears and sliding down his neck.

* * *

SEVERAL weeks after Fakeer took Sannyas, Bhagwan left for a meditation camp in the foothills of the Himalayas. Fakeer packed up his few possessions and followed him there. You could be closer to Bhagwan at these smaller retreats. Without the crowds of the city, you were able to sit in small groups at his feet while he spoke. The journey to camp was a three-day train ride from the city, without a seat, standing and swaying with the movement of the car on the tracks. Blisteringly hot and inhumanely crowded. Fakeer slept standing up with his head resting on an arm that gripped the worn leather ceiling strap. When the train came to a shuddering, knee-buckling stop at a station along the route, he exited the train, buying food on the platform from the sellers who crowded the stations. Metal trays called thalis were filled with chickpeas, vegetable curry and naan and covered in a thick sauce spiced with cumin, mustard seeds and saffron. Fakeer would crouch on the crowded train platform with the rest of the travelers from the train and eat. Watching a businessman's shoes passing quickly or a beggar with a limp in their step. Sandals ground down on the inside of the heel. The food was like eating fire, gut churning, perspiration dampening his newly dyed clothes. Sudden rivulets of crimson sweat running down his back. Then the bell would ring and everyone would rush to return the metal trays and board the train again. Out of the window the mountains began to push up from the flat earth, their distant snow-capped peaks signaling his arrival. When Fakeer disembarked in the small village where Bhagwan was staying, he rented a small room for a couple of dollars and collapsed. Ragged and sleeping where he fell.

★ ★ ★

At the camp, mornings were filled with meditation, cooking and cleaning. It was a hermitic, solitary existence spent in silent contemplation. Disciples of Bhagwan paid their way by working at the camp communally. Fakeer washed dishes, swept floors and scrubbed toilets. He cut vegetables in the big, sun-filled kitchen for large communal lunches. Everyone ate together at small tables, talking softly. The afternoons were for the groups that were a central tenet in Bhagwan's teachings. Intense, week-long sessions of laughter, screaming and sorrow. Furiously recasting past family trauma or playing games like children full of laughing wonder. Weeping and dancing. The setting sun throwing the purple-black shadows of the ancient mountains across the dirt. In the evenings, everyone walked in an ambling caravan to the camp's outdoor pavilion to listen to Bhagwan speak. Cold stars blinking across the Southern Hemisphere's night sky above them. Sannyasins sitting, alone and in groups, on a hard-packed dirt floor in a rough semicircle at the master's feet. A reverential silence blowing through like the cool mountain air. For Fakeer, it was almost too powerful to be so close to Bhagwan's presence. His brilliance was like an electric jolt, incredibly painful and beautiful and joyous. His words were like a fire, a suffering and a celebration. Destroying everything that was false, leaving Fakeer with only himself. Here, Fakeer felt more deeply himself than he ever had. He had arrived in India lost and had finally been found. His people, his purpose was here at the dusty feet of the Himalayas.

★ ★ ★

A large part of Fakeer's new meditation practice was focused on healing his rift with his parents. He still remained deeply divided in his feelings for his parents, especially his father. In meditation he would howl and dance and create scenes where he would scream at his dad until spittle flecked his jaw and he had made himself hoarse. Even with this work, he maintained feelings of shame and worthlessness coupled with a vengeful anger. But his work at the commune, his meditation practice and Bhagwan finally began to give him space to breathe. In this space, his mental health felt less precarious, and it opened a place in his heart for the child he was about to have and for the life in front of him. He came to the realization that he could do better than his parents had done. He would be the father he never had.

One morning the mail carrier on a diesel motorbike informed him that a letter had arrived for him at the town's small post office. After prepping lunch, Fakeer walked to the postal building that sat on a sloping hill at the edge of town. An old postmaster with a short gray beard that had been dipped in henna and burned a bright orange worked inside. He wearily found the letter and with a curious look handed Fakeer the creased envelope. It had been forwarded from the Rex in the city and his friend's apartment before that. Inky stamps scattered a shifting chronology across the front of the envelope. A light dread settled into the pit of Fakeer's stomach; he knew it was time to go back. He was determined to be there for the baby, but his hands were shaking as he looked over the letter. *Please Stanley, please come back for your baby's birth. I don't want to do this alone. I've started to have early contractions and the doctor says it could be any day now.* He sat on the small rickety bench out front and read DuShaun's sloping, desperate print over and over again, a creeping despair slowly crawling up the back of his sunburned neck. He looked around and then stood up and quickly walked back to his room, pushing his anxiety to the pit of his stomach. In his room, he immediately began packing, afraid that if he waited, he would lose the courage to go. Shaking off his uncertainty, he became newly determined to somehow make this little family work. The next morning, without telling anyone, he caught the train heading back to Bombay. Standing in the packed aisle watching the village pull away.

Arm hooked in the crook of a strap. Crouched on the platform, shoveling fire into his belly. Sweat-stained. Finally pulling into the ornate Victoria Terminus train station, with its iconic vaulted ceilings and colonialist architecture. Under the glass domes, he shouldered his bag with the broken zipper and flew back to Ohio.

Chapter Six

LOOKING BACK NOW, THIS TIME WAS ONE OF GREAT HOPE for my mother. She was naive enough to be optimistic and still clung to the belief that love and perseverance would carry them through. When Fakeer came back as he had promised, DuShaun was thrilled and hugely relieved. Her dream of a family was held together with paste. She wasn't enthusiastic about his newfound master and the red and orange clothing, but he seemed happier so she let it slide. DuShaun had always questioned the Christianity she had been brought up with, and Fakeer was now completely unmoored from the Jewish faith of his childhood. So DuShaun put her faith in the two of them and the baby she believed would make them whole.

Fakeer had only been home a week when my mother started having intense contractions. It had been raining steadily all that day, the raindrops hitting the windows of the hospital's oppressive waiting room, where Fakeer had been forced to sit. DuShaun's birth was long, and Fakeer had not been allowed into the room where she was laboring. Separated from him, she bore down with the help of the nurses. Out in the waiting room, Fakeer railed against the archaic and sexist hospital policy but was rebuffed by a manager in a brown suit and tie. When I was finally born and DuShaun was resting, a nurse brought me out for Fakeer to see. When he reached out to take his child in his arms, the old crone slapped his hands away. She looked at the dirty hippie in front of her as if he were contagious. He demanded to be given his daughter and she eventually relented, but only after he went and washed his hands, furious. Fakeer took me in his arms and couldn't help but grin, relieved to feel affection and love for this new little creature. DuShaun was eager to get me back home, so the new parents left Springfield General a couple of days later and headed back to the farm.

DuShaun was thrilled to be a mother. Having assumed for so long that she would never have the chance, she now relished every moment. Finally, something that was hers amid the maelstrom of her family. At the hospital they encouraged her to use formula, and she didn't know enough to breastfeed. So back at the farm, she held me gently and stared into my eyes as I took the bottle. During the first few weeks, Doreen would come onto the porch and lay down on the mattress next to the two of us, cooing at me and kissing my cheeks. After twenty-five years, she had only recently stopped working for the family for whom she had cooked, cleaned and raised children. She wouldn't admit it, but Doreen had been feeling sick for several years and she was starting to rapidly deteriorate. In the winter they would diagnose her with ovarian cancer and she would be gone by spring. Doreen had birthed, raised and fed fifteen children while also working a grueling job. She had been brutally tough on her kids when they were younger, but she had also been funny, highly intelligent and had passed along her love of reading. Her death was a huge blow to her family, and DuShaun mourned her for years. But for the moment, the two women sat together, happily playing with me.

DuShaun also leaned heavily on her twin, Joann, who would stop by often with her two young daughters, bringing formula and hand-me-down clothes. Fakeer was unprepared and overwhelmed but still determined to make things right. He missed the ashram in India and Bhagwan desperately but stayed resolute in his commitment to his new family. To maintain a connection to the person he was in India, he listened to Bhagwan speaking on cassette while he practiced sunrise dynamic meditation in the back field. The Walkers once again gathered at the window, Alonzo left shaking his head at the "crazy white boy" while having his morning coffee and cigar. After a lifetime of wild nights, beautiful women and hard physical labor, Alonzo had also begun to slow down. In the end, he was the one who took care of Doreen as she died, holding her hand gently and listening to her prayers. "Dotty, you ain't got nothing to pray about, you already got me here." His failing lungs would take him two years later.

My parents named me Anais, after Anaïs Nin, whom they were both reading at the time. Library copies of her diaries sat water-stained and dog-eared, piled beside diapers and infant formula. They chose Anais because Nin was a feminist icon who wrote scandalous erotica and had many love affairs, most famously with Henry Miller and his wife, June, which she wrote about at length in *Henry and June*. She chose a life lived in full and with abandon. "We don't see things as they are, we see things as we are," she famously quoted from the Talmud. All Fakeer and DuShaun could see were dreams deferred as they still yearned to live life fully, to create something different than what they had grown up with. In those first few weeks they chose a name that might work a little magic. A talisman to buffer against the shrinking opportunities for a life well lived. But as the summer wore on, they realized magic wasn't going to find us on a leaky front porch on a crowded farm in Ohio.

★ ★ ★

WHEN I was four months old, as fall turned the Ohio buckeyes wilted and brown, Fakeer decided he wanted to live closer to other Sannyasins. He was also emphatic that he didn't want me raised around any family members who could be so violent with their kids. My mother was not particularly interested in Bhagwan or becoming one of his disciples, but she saw that it made Fakeer more stable and she was intent on keeping her family together. Without her own compass or a plan, she agreed to follow Fakeer across the country.

With a new baby in tow, my parents struck out for California, where they could be near a large commune that had formed there. Our family drove across the country and eventually arrived in San Mateo. My father knew several Sannyasins from his time in India and they helped us find an apartment near the commune. California in 1973 was in a period of deep unrest and fear. The economy was faltering and the oil crisis was battering the job market. There was also a deep suspicion of cults and their followers after several gruesome murders. The Manson murders had happened just a few years before, and down the street from our apartment, Jim Jones—the fiery leader of the Peoples Temple—was making news. At that time, the temple was in the initial stages of preparing its followers for their ill-fated and murderous move to Guyana. These violent cults and their deification of troubled leaders brought mistrust down on the commune and the community my mother and father were joining.

It was in the middle of all of this that my parents got

married in a simple ceremony in Walnut Creek, a town across the bay outside of Oakland. It was a small gathering, a few friends from the commune and the hippie Unitarian minister who married them. My father had an uncle-in-law who lived in the area whom he saw sporadically but he didn't bother to invite him. My mother was wearing a white thrift-store dress and my father wore jeans, a vest and tie. I was a chubby-cheeked baby in diapers, with black curly hair and a big smile. After the ceremony, the small wedding party walked to a hill overlooking the bay and laid out a potluck lunch. Basking in the glow of a toast to the new couple, Fakeer and DuShaun dared to be hopeful on that sunny day, surrounded by new friends.

★ ★ ★

DESPITE their hope, the newlyweds struggled to find work to support themselves and their new baby in a new city. My dad eventually found a job as a security guard at the *San Francisco Chronicle*, just as Patty Hearst, heiress to the paper's fortune, engaged in a bloody criminal spectacle that engulfed the area. His days were spent fending off reporters at the Mission Street headquarters or taking naps in the basement staff room. At night he worked in an electronics store where he would steal the odd portable stereo to pawn when things were especially tight. My mother also worked two jobs, as a representative for AAA and a department store clerk. At AAA, she was a phone trip clerk who would plan itineraries for families driving across the country. Booking motels in Florida and sightseeing tours in New York City. Places she could only dream of going. Her nights were spent restocking shelves in the department store and fending off advances from her boss. She worried constantly about whether I was being looked after properly by the teenage babysitter they could barely afford.

At the commune, Fakeer started doing meditation groups again with several other disciples of Bhagwan. He also began to get deeply involved in the primal therapy that was newly starting up there. Primal therapy was a raw and painful self-flagellation that involved screaming and lashing out physically. It was psychologically brutal and the long sessions left him emotionally reeling. In India, his meditation practice had brought him a semblance of peace, but this primal therapy threatened to disrupt his delicate balance. He began to attend sessions daily and his mental health and the mood at home soon darkened. Because of his family connection and worsening mental health, he had begun to see his uncle-in-law, who was a psychotherapist. He was also in sporadic touch with his mother, when she called to check in on them, but Fakeer was still not speaking with his father.

It was a few months before my first birthday when I received the Hindu name Ma Yoga Puja, which means "to worship." And even though my mother remained skeptical,

DuShaun also took Sannyas, becoming Ma Pradeepa. Although she was much more ambivalent about being a Sannyasin than Fakeer, she was intent on keeping her husband happy. But the cracks were starting to show. While Fakeer was becoming more devout, she would surreptitiously change out of her red and orange clothing before heading to work and often meditated with one eye open. She was suspicious of all these liberal white people and resented Fakeer spending more time at the commune than he did at home. After her time at Antioch, which she'd spent among a group of multicultural friends, Pradeepa had again become more withdrawn. As part of the only interracial couple in their circle, my mother was often the sole person of color in a completely white community. She felt insecure around all of these California blonds with their lithe frames and entitled attitudes. People reached out to touch her hair and commented on their surprise that she could tan. They presented as progressive but carried the same breezy, dismissive attitudes toward race and equality as the people she'd grown up with, and they slowly undercut her belief in her place there. At the same time, unbeknownst to Pradeepa, Fakeer was beginning to rapidly spiral into depression and despair. Becoming more desperate as he tried to manage work, a new baby and the intensity of primal therapy. As Pradeepa became angrier and more displaced, Fakeer became more emotionally erratic, and they continued to struggle financially and as partners.

Downstairs in the small compound where we rented a one-bedroom apartment, trouble had moved in. A group of rednecks from Pennsylvania had recently taken over a couple of apartments and filled the parking lot with Harley-Davidson motorcycles. They were loud and had late-night parties where fights and shouting were common. They were immediately suspicious of my parents, an interracial couple, and their mixed-race baby who all seemed to be part of some cult. They would often mutter derogatory comments at my mother, and late one night a rock was thrown through our apartment window. Fakeer confronted them, and a physical confrontation that was only going to end badly for him was averted after Pradeepa called the police.

And then, out of the blue, Phil and Shirley called and asked if they could visit us in California for my first birthday. My mother saved for weeks to buy groceries and on the night they were coming she put out cheese and Ritz crackers as hors d'oeuvres. She set the small table with their best mismatched plates and cutlery and cooked a fancy dinner they couldn't afford. She was determined to impress my father's parents and show them what a good wife and mother she was, despite what they thought of her. Fakeer hadn't spoken with his father since shortly after they told him about the pregnancy. Now, full of an impenetrable rage and chafing under the yolk of poverty, he was desperate to get his parents' financial and emotional help but bristling at having to beg for it.

What my parents didn't know was that, weeks earlier, Phil had received a call from an in-law he hadn't heard from in years, the psychotherapist in San Francisco. After dispensing with the obligatory chat about marriages and dead family members, the therapist got to the point of his call. He had been giving Stanley free medical appointments because he felt sorry for him and because he was family. But my father had recently been talking about wanting to kill himself and it made the therapist uncomfortable. He thought Phil should know so that he could get his son some help. Shocked and embarrassed, Phil apologized and assured him that he would take care of it.

When they arrived at the apartment, Shirley immediately picked me up and held me gently in her arms. Asking my mother about how I was doing and what I had been eating. My mother proudly informed her that I was growing beautifully. Phil stood at the front door, looking around, disgust clear on his face. He entered the dingy apartment as the rock music blared from the apartment below. My mother had cleaned and mopped for the better part of the day but there was no hiding the water-stained walls and filthy, worn-down carpet.

"How can you live this way?" Phil simmered. "What are you doing with your life, Stanley?"

"My name is Fakeer." My father had been bracing for a confrontation all day; his newfound spiritual freedom and mental instability had created a wild rage and sneering contempt for his parents' conformity. His internal conflict caused him to lash out and verbally antagonize his father, bringing an already heated situation to a boil. Furious at the humiliation of a family member having seen his son this way, Phil shouted at Fakeer. "You're an embarrassment. We didn't raise you like this!"

"You didn't raise me at all, old man! You think you've got some kind of fucking moral authority here?!"

Erupting, Phil slapped Fakeer across the face and my father became physical, taking his father down to the ground. They continued to wrestle on the frayed rug while my grandmother and mother shrieked and cried, begging them to stop. Phil and Shirley left the apartment quickly after that. Shirley handed me back to my mother with a quick kiss on the head. There was an agonized glance at her son and then they were gone. They wouldn't speak again for a year.

* * *

FAKEER stopped seeing his uncle-in-law and went deeper into primal therapy. He was searching for what he had glimpsed in India, that sense of meaning and place. But, maddeningly, it seemed to be getting further away. His mental health continued to deteriorate and he was fired from the electronics store after the owners discovered his stealing. A few months later, my mom's boss laid her off after she gruffly and finally rebuffed his lewd advances. The job at AAA did not pay enough to cover their bills, and now they couldn't even scrape up enough money to make their $300 rent. The neighbors had become more menacing and they felt under threat from every angle. Out of options, they packed up the car and headed back across country after a year and a half on the West Coast. There was no itinerary for Pradeepa to plan, no sights to see on the way.

They were beat and busted and had to retreat to Ohio on their last tank of gas. We spent the next couple of years there. We lived with my aunt Joann, who had recently had her third daughter, in her small apartment and on the farm. Doreen had died that spring and Alonzo was now getting sick, so my mom collected welfare and helped look after her ailing father. From that time, I remember days spent at the farm with my many cousins. The broken and undulating stone path leading to the screened-in porch. All of us swinging on the tire hanging from a frayed yellow rope tied to the massive Ohio buckeye that shaded the tall grass in the front yard. The worn Chantilly lace curtains stirring in the warm breeze. These are only shards of memories from this time, but they have stayed with me.

In 1976, when I was three, Fakeer returned to Toronto, where he could work legally and anchor a new life for our family. He found an apartment for the three of us to live in and got a job driving a taxi. Pradeepa had been shaken by their time in California and was wary of moving to another country where she would again have no support system and openly hostile in-laws. But after her father died and the farm was sold, she was bereft and determined anew to keep her marriage together. She still loved this man and would follow him to Canada, looking to start again.

Chapter Seven

I N 1976, TORONTO WAS A CONSERVATIVE BACKWATER JUST starting to go through the social convulsions that would shake it down to its white, protestant roots. Immigrants had begun to reshape the city in their multicultural and diverse image, but it was still unquestionably conservative and protestant. We lived in Parkdale, a landing pad for new Canadians and home to generations of people living in poverty. The winter we arrived was the coldest since Environment Canada started keeping records. The city was frigid and blasted with snow and sleet that rattled our windows. I remember the air in our small apartment smelled of stale frying oil from the restaurant below. My mother had to shove towels under the doors to keep the mice out. To keep our small family afloat, my mom worked as a waitress, under the table, in a restaurant down the block and my dad drove a cab for Beck Taxi. I remember it was chaotic and insecure; my parents were working poor and we all felt the grind of it.

My father had been in contact with his parents sporadically following the disastrous California visit, and after moving back to Toronto, my father and I went to visit them a few times. The visits were always short and filled with tension around the fact that my mother was not welcome. I remember riding in the taxi up the long driveway and looking out over the rolling hills as if I were in some kind of dream. We would stand in the kitchen while my grandmother touched my cheek and held my hand and asked my dad confusing questions: "How long are you going to keep this up?" and "How can you stay in something so unstable?" Sometimes my grandfather would come home, and the temperature in the room would immediately change with the sound of his car pulling up. My dad would quickly scoop me up and we would leave hastily, my grandmother stealing kisses as we left. When we returned to our cramped apartment my mother would busy herself, tensely inquiring how it went. "Did you ask them for help?"

My dad would respond angrily. "They're not going to do that. I told you, this is my mess."

My mother turning on him. "I'm not anyone's mess!"

I knew enough to make myself scarce at that point, as their fights were always loudest after those visits. I began to dread going to that big house, the strange tension, knowing what would come afterward. My mother begged Fakeer to ask them for financial help so we could move into a better apartment, but he refused, insisting we would make it on our own.

★ ★ ★

WHEN I was four, my mother found me a spot at a daycare for low-income kids at the local YMCA. The YMCA was one of Canada's largest charities, and it focused on social issues like poverty and inequality. This particular chapter ran a daycare and gym that was a socialist experiment in helping low-income kids access programs and create some stability. The daycare was housed inside of a large red-brick building from the 1800s with high arches at its entrance. For me and my neighborhood daycare friends, it was a refuge from our complicated situations at home. The people looking after us were young and sometimes sketchy, but they basically left us to do what we wanted.

In the center of the daycare was an adult-sized wooden dollhouse, large enough for rooms we could play in and featuring a second floor. The rooms had been furnished with donated furniture and random household goods. In the play kitchen, there were aprons and pots and pans from the local Goodwill store. We used the pots to cook elaborate meals, our stove a table with burners drawn on with marker. Someone had sewn curtains out of fabric with a bright red-and-orange flower pattern and hung them above all the window cutouts. The bedrooms had beds with pillows and sheets and a dresser in each. In the living room there was a couch and even a working black-and-white television that got two channels. The daycare kids, of every conceivable shade, culture and background, quickly established a family hierarchy. We played house passionately, as if in some futile attempt to create stable familial ties and rules. Left to ourselves for hours, my wife and I cooked, argued, chastised the kids and even shared kisses in the "parent" bedroom. It was a relief to come from our chaotic homes to the relatively structured family we created for ourselves in the massive dollhouse.

* * *

My mom worked nights so my dad was supposed to pick me up from daycare at the end of every day. I was often the last kid there. I remember waiting late into the evenings as the underpaid, endlessly patient daycare worker checked her watch. It was sad and lonely, and I hated seeing the other kids leave. When my dad would arrive, harried and exhausted after driving a cab all day, I would run to him, elated. Never sure until the moment he rounded the corner when he was actually going to show up. But he always did, no matter how late, tired or broke. He would run up the stairs, apologizing to the daycare worker, and wrap me in his arms. "You ready, kid?"

We would walk out into the bracingly cold night and pile into his orange-and-green cab and go to Mars Diner on College Street. Mars Diner was an old-school joint downtown where taxi drivers hung out on their breaks drinking coffee. Every night I would order a hot chocolate and one of their famous corn bread muffins for dinner. I loved sitting with my dad and his taxi buddies at the counter while they exchanged stories and commiserated. The older cabbies, who were mainly from Poland and Romania, would rib my long-haired dad who dressed in red, orange and pink. My dad would sit next to me and ask me about my day and I would hold his hand. I noticed he seemed to smile more these days, to be present and joking with me in a way that he hadn't before. I loved those nights out when it was just the two of us.

But things at home were steadily deteriorating: my parents were exhausted, fighting endlessly over unpaid bills and dashed dreams. My father still yearned to return to India but my mother had never taken to being a Sannyasin. Soon after we moved to Toronto she changed her name back to Jean and stopped wearing orange and red; I found her mala stashed away in her drawer. My mother was working hard to establish us here and my father still believed that his purpose was in India. Without friends or family in Toronto, my mother turned to me as

I got older, and I became her confidant. On the days that I wasn't at daycare we would wander the city and sit outside of attractions we couldn't afford to go into. We visited the outside of the Royal Ontario Museum and the Toronto Art Gallery, and we stood at the bottom of the CN Tower. She and I would talk about her troubles and my parents' relationship. She began to call me Ma, a short-form of Ma Yoga Puja, but it came to mean something else. She was my mom and I was her ma. Both parenting one another. Although I was proud that I was treated as an equal, it was also scary being privy to the issues in an adult relationship that felt so fundamental to my survival. I felt a responsibility to help protect my mother and carry the burdens she was struggling with, but I also just wanted her to be able to take care of me. To parent me and not ask to be parented in return. We were each other's best friends, daughters and mothers, and the constant switching between roles confused me.

At night, I lay awake on my bed on the couch in the living room and listened to my parents arguing. It was often loud, and it was incredibly scary to hear them verbally attack one another so viciously. I could drown most of it out if I covered my head with a blanket and squeezed my ears tightly. But the base notes of their fury still resonated. I began to notice that, outside of those fights, they didn't seem to talk to each other anymore. The summer I turned five, things finally imploded and my dad told us he was returning to

India. My mother issued a warning: "If you leave this time don't bother coming back. I swear to God, Stanley."

He bristled; she only called him Stanley when she wanted to piss him off. "I can't be with you anymore. I don't love you. I want out," he told her.

In the morning, he packed his bag and walked into the living room and knelt down beside me. He sighed and gave me a kiss on the cheek as I pretended to sleep. "Look, kid, I'm sorry. I've gotta go. I promise I'm coming back. It's just going to be for a while." He stood, and I could feel he was looking at me, but I refused to open my eyes. Then he was gone.

For the next few days I sat forlornly at the window, waiting for him to come back. If my mother caught me there waiting, she would get angry and tell me not to waste my time. "It's just the two of us now and you'd better get used to it. That man is nothing to us."

As the days wore on a cold dread settled in the pit of my stomach as I realized my dad was truly gone, leaving me alone with my mother, who was growing increasingly erratic. After Fakeer split, my mother went dark for a couple months. She sat for hours on the couch staring into space, heartbroken. At six years old, I began to walk myself the couple of blocks home from daycare. I would come in to find Jean hadn't moved since I had left that morning. We watched a lot of television, mostly cartoons and game shows, and ate a lot of fast food. I could tell she was trying to keep it together, make a meal every once in a while, and be loving. She was just so sad and lost and she couldn't hide it. Whenever I tried to speak of my father, to ask when we would see him again, she would become furious, unable to hear his name without it setting her off.

I remember feeling completely alone in my grief and buried under the weight of my mother's anger. She tried to keep her waitressing job but was fired when she didn't show up for work several days in a row. Eventually we went on welfare. When we couldn't afford our meager rent above the restaurant, we moved into a crumbling rooming house in an even sketchier neighborhood. Every night I could hear people ranting in their rooms next door as my mom and I slept on a mattress on the wooden floor together. She wept through the night, stalked by fear, depression and instability. I lay in the warm curve of her body, a stone of anxiety settling in my gut. I felt abandoned by my father, whom I loved and missed terribly. Without him we were sinking, and I realized I would have to hang on to survive.

★ ★ ★

As spring finally came to the city that year, the staff at the YMCA daycare started taking us to the Adventure Playground down at Harbourfront. Harbourfront was an area at the southernmost tip of the city, on the shores of Lake Ontario. It was a collection of trees, paths and big empty parking lots sandwiched between an expressway and the lake. In one of these unused fields, the City of Toronto had started a kids' program. Adventure Playground was a massive building area for kids filled with a collection of lumber, tools, wooden blocks, truck tires and paint. The city also collected and delivered piles of wood that were scattered around the field. Hundreds of tools were stored in buckets: hammers, saws, screwdrivers, and thousands of nails in large coffee tins. Cans of colored paint and every size of paintbrush were also stacked and ready to be put to use.

Every week we would board the public bus outside the daycare and the staff would take a rambunctious dozen of us down to the Adventure Playground. We would troop off the bus and, whooping and hollering, run for the wooden structures. After the daycare staff signed us in, they would head off to smoke and hang out. We kids were set loose to build and create what we wanted. Without adult supervision. In fact, adults were expressly *not* allowed, according to the hand-painted sign at the entrance. *Children Only. No Adults Allowed!* With hours on hand, my friends and I would saw, hammer and nail together teetering two- and even three-story structures. Precariously high floors that were thrilling to put together. Ladders were ingeniously built so that we could reach the higher stories of our buildings. The top floors were often so high that we had a clear and glorious view of Lake Ontario. Large naval ships would sometimes sail by, and we would wave flags furiously like pirate stowaways until the ship let out a huge blast, to our absolute crowing delight. We would paint truck tires wet with color and pile them as high as we could, saw and hammer plywood into huge, crumbling art sculptures.

Each week was a chance to add to the tunnels and shacks that we had connected by rope and plank bridges the days and weeks before. "Regulars only! Back off!" we would bellow at curious kids who would come by for an hour and dare try to enter our buildings. Tilting at crooked windmills and sailing wooden-block boats on freshly painted blue metal waves. A fantastical world without adults, where we feral kids dreamed and built our own intricate community. Sometimes a rain storm would gather purple and bruised on the horizon and then eventually blow in off the lake in sheets. All of the kids would take shelter together, laughing and shivering in our handmade lean-tos. We huddled around several firepits that the adults would get going and occasionally come by to stoke, but mostly left to the kids to keep roaring by feeding in lengths of wood. The rain beat down on the corrugated metal roofs and sunk our discarded tools in the mud. As the storm raged around us, we sheltered in a world we had created for ourselves.

In those hidden, musty spaces, I found a place away from the chaos and anxiety I was facing at home. I remember one of the kids I knew but didn't build with very often began to cry one afternoon under leaden skies. As the fire flickered in front of us, he sat weeping openly and angrily, wiping at his face with his dirty hands until he left streaks. No one said anything; we just gathered around him murmuring words of encouragement and laying our hands on his back or arm. His crying finally subsided and we all went back to our places around the pit. No one made fun or called him out. We knew we were all fighting our own battles. I was still heartbroken that my dad had left and that weeks would go by without me hearing from him. I was constantly worried that my mom might not be able to find her footing again and we would continue to free fall. But my natural disposition was one of enthusiastic excitement about life and it was given full expression here.

★ ★ ★

"DEMOLITION Day! Demolition Day!"

The kids chanted as the young guys on the staff played bongos with their shirts off. All tan skin and white teeth. It was Demolition Day on our last visit to Adventure Playground before it would close for the season. Awards were given out for "Best Fort" and tug-of-war contests were waged in the center of the playground. Then, the drum beat began to grow ominous and we began to shout, "Destroy it all! Tear it down!" raising our crowbars and hammers in the air. A homemade tin horn was ceremoniously blown and we ran to rip down the structures we had so painstakingly built. Tearing our dreams and plans to tatters until we staggered back exhausted and sweaty. The denouement of the day was when the staff attached long ropes to the top of the tallest structure in the playground, three or four stories tall. We formed lines and grabbed hold of the ropes. "One, two, three, pull!" All the kids and counselors pulled on the ropes in unison, rocking the massive structure. "Again! Pull!" Another huge pull and the structure teetered with an apocalyptic creak, seemed like it was going to right itself and then came crashing to the ground in a huge cloud of dust, coating us all in bits of wood and a tsunami of dirt. Extraordinarily dangerous. Completely amazing.

* * *

A couple of months after my father left, at my mother's lowest point financially and emotionally, she was contacted by an agency that she had signed up with through the YMCA. It was a resource that helped newly arrived low-income women find a job and file for a working visa in the country. They found my mother a temporary position in a women's shelter down the street from us. It was a tough, demanding job, but it helped her get on her feet and gave her some renewed sense of purpose. She was working with women who were battling addiction or fleeing an abusive living situation, and it suited her. She threw herself into the work and began to get a regular paycheck for the first time since arriving in Toronto.

Chapter Eight

IT WAS DURING THIS TIME THAT MY GRANDMOTHER, Shirley, called and asked if she could see me. Shirley eventually told me that when my dad left for India, she realized we were in trouble and tracked us down. This wasn't an easy feat, as we had moved from our apartment and were still living in the rooming house, where we didn't have our own phone. There was a telephone line in the entryway to the building and most people used that. One day someone shouted up the stairs: "Jean, call for you!"

I went out to our hallway, which overlooked the entrance, and watched through the banister spindles as my mother picked up the receiver. I could see her jaw tense and a look of anger pass over her features. I knew it was that lady again and it scared me. It reminded me of how my mom would get after my visits to the big house with my dad, and I knew it was going to upset her. But this time I wouldn't have my dad as a buffer and I feared having to face the recriminations alone. I could see her finishing up the phone call below me, could hear her tightly agreeing to a time and place that she wrote on a flyer stuffed into one of the mailboxes. She hung up looking heavy, having made a Faustian bargain. She looked up and caught me sitting there so she came up and sat beside me.

I shook my head. "No way. I'm not going!"

"You gotta get to know them," she insisted, which I just found more confusing.

"She doesn't even know us, mama."

"Listen here, Ma. This might be a way for you to know a life outside the broke-ass limited resources I grew up with. You've got a chance to see some of the things I couldn't."

"I don't want to go up there without you again," I pleaded. "It's scary."

My mother took my hand and looked at me sadly. "Puja, I don't want you to go either, but we don't have a pot to piss in or a window to throw it out of. There are some things you gotta do, I gotta do, and this is one of them."

"You should come with me ," I said accusingly, and she let my hand go.

"This is your family, and I'm sorry, child, but you're going to have to do this alone."

The next morning she put me in a little flowered dress

and I cleaned my scuffed running shoes. We danced to Aretha Franklin and ate Froot Loops in our room with the mattress on the floor. Then we left the rooming house and together we took the bus to the Ossington subway station, a dirty and drab metro stop that connected us to the rest of the city. We got on the graffitied subway car and took it fourteen stops, heading first east and then north, switching at the Yonge Street station and eventually arriving at York Mills. From there we got on another bus and rode another eight stops until we got off on the side of a wide road.

In the north end of the city new roads were being built like highways, huge thoroughfares six lanes across with wide shoulders along the sides. My stomach was already feeling queasy and nervous by the time we spotted my grandmother waiting to pick me up. She was sitting behind the steering wheel of her salmon-colored Cadillac looking tense. She would later say, "I saw you get off the bus and you looked just like your father." When she and my grandfather had first been told about Jean's pregnancy they had been incensed, convinced my mother had tricked their teenage son into it for their money. But more sear- ingly, they were both heartbroken that their first grand- child would not be Jewish, and they blamed my mother for that loss. From the beginning they were both adamant that she wouldn't receive a penny from them. But once I was born, Shirley saw the child in the middle of all of those harsh and angry words and began to soften. With

Phil still unwilling to help his son and wife, Shirley decided that she would have to see me herself.

After that first stay, I began to visit my grandmother more regularly. During those early visits, I would start my day sitting at the counter while Shirley prepared a full-course breakfast in the salmon-colored kitchen that matched her car. Eggs and sausages fried on the stove while she cut up a fresh fruit salad from scratch. She would make a pot of tea and I would ask her to tell me stories about my dad. I loved hearing her tales about him as a naughty kid. Her memories made me feel connected to him, and I remember realizing that my grandmother and I were both missing the same person. She had also lost Fakeer. I very rarely brought up my dad's absence at home with my mother. She was still furious and heartbroken about the way he'd left and any remarks about him were met with an angry grief. With Shirley, it was different. We happily and eagerly talked about him and how much we loved him and how goofy and wonderful and totally irresponsible he could be. Whenever one of us got a creased and stamped letter from India we would share it with the other. She was a connection to him and I loved her for it.

During the rest of the day, my grandmother and I would sit at the large dining table and make crafts from macaroni and toilet paper tubes she had collected and saved for my visits. We glued and talked about what I was learning in school and she would tell me about her days as a child in a one-room schoolhouse downtown. A row of hospitals had been built up around it, but the school was still there, an anachronism sitting in their shade. Some afternoons I would get dressed in my new clothes that I kept at my grandmother's house and join her on errands to the grocery store and the kosher butcher. We'd chat with the other Jewish ladies at her weekly hair appointment. Her hairdresser once, unwisely, attempted to straighten my curly hair. I immediately sweated it out, turning it into a frizzy halo that I thought was dazzlingly glamorous. Shirley wasn't affectionate with me necessarily, but she was steadfast and funny and I grew to like her immensely. When I was with her she was the adult in the room and I was the child. I came to realize I could trust that she meant what she said and would be where she promised. After the chaos of my parents, it was a huge relief to rely on someone so unwavering. I very rarely saw my grandfather though; when I was there he was almost always at work during the day and would often come home after I had gone to bed. I was still nervous around him, and he accepted my presence with a resigned ambivalence.

★ ★ ★

WHEN I was eight, in 1981, my grandparents and I began to go for Sunday dinner at the Primrose Club. The Primrose Club was a swishy private Jewish social club on a midtown street, St. Clair Avenue, where the valets helped us out of our car when we arrived. Inside, we stopped at the coat check and Shirley left her ankle-length fur coat with the attendant. For my first visit, I was wearing a velvet-trimmed dress from the closet in my room and new shiny shoes that pinched my feet. Shirley gave me a final once-over with approval and took Phil's arm. Then we climbed the staircase and entered a massive dining room overlooking the twinkling lights of the city below. I had an impression of all-dark wainscotting and marble, offset by white tablecloths and shined silverware reflecting the soft light from the overhead chandeliers. Old-school waiters wore tuxedos and white gloves and knew my grandparents by name. It all felt so impossibly sophisticated.

My grandparents' table was strategically located on the far side of the room, so the walk to the table was epic and exhilarating. My grandparents were so glamorous that it felt like all eyes were on our arrival. I was proud to be with them and walked with my little head held high. Once we were seated, other guests approached my grandfather to ask for an audience or to commend him on a recent donation to a Jewish charity. He was powerful and connected, and everyone knew it. He made the rounds in the room like a newly elected politician with a suave Sinatra vibe. My grandmother, coral lipstick perfectly applied, played the part of his loyal spouse. When the inevitable question arose—who was this little brown girl?—my grandfather fell uncharacteristically quiet. Shirley didn't equivocate: she introduced me as their granddaughter without hesitation. She had a direct look in her eye that I came to learn warned her interlocutor against being indiscreet. I noticed the flash of surprise across people's features, quickly replaced by tight smiles and good manners. I wasn't embarrassed by their attitudes—they were unfailingly polite and complimented me on how "cute" I was—but it made me acutely aware of the shape-shifting that was once again required in order to fit in. It reminded me that the rules in this world didn't necessarily benefit a little Black girl like me, so I was going to have to learn them quickly.

But I think more than anything, I just wanted my grandparents to be proud of me. So I listened intently as my grandmother taught me which silverware to use and how to lay a cloth napkin across my lap. How to sit up straight and look people in the eye. Then the meal arrived. This became the part that I looked forward to all week. Each course was served by several waiters who revealed the food from under a silver cloche, accompanied by a puff of steam. Dinner began with matzo ball soup (soon my favorite), then brisket and potatoes covered in gravy, and finally Jell-O for dessert. I loved every minute of it, reveling in the glamour and in the fiction that I belonged. Some nights I'd return home to my mother from the Primrose Club carrying doggy bags, having changed back into my old clothes.

My mother would get indignant when I tried to give the food to her. "I don't need their damn leftovers. Who do you think I am? We're not a charity case." I would backpedal: "I know, Ma. I just saved some 'cause I thought you might want to try it." Then she would throw it in the garbage. "Well, you thought wrong."

She had wanted me to know my father's family, but every time I returned I felt her simmering rage at being excluded. She knew it wasn't my fault, but I could tell by the way she looked at me that she hated me a little for it anyway. I always lied and told her how much I hated my Bridle Path visits, and she would eventually, gratefully believe me. The two of us would curl up on the couch and watch *Sunday Night Football*. We loved the Pittsburgh Steelers and they were having another rough season that year, so we cheered them mightily. We were happy to just be together again. The next morning, I would find the food containers back on the counter, empty.

* * *

THESE visits and dinners had been going on for some time, and I was beginning to settle into my Bridle Path role. Until one Sunday evening, at the end of one of our Primrose dinners, I stood waiting by the downstairs kitchen that served the club's ballroom as my grandmother collected her coat from the coat-check girl and my grandfather finished shaking hands in the dining room. Bored, I wandered down the hallway toward the loud music. Through a door I watched a bar mitzvah taking place in the ballroom. The room was packed and the bar mitzvah boy was being lifted up on a chair, a bright spotlight on him as he was passed around the room. Music pulsing, his family dancing and sweating in a joyous circle beneath him. I had never seen a kid have such an exuberant celebration of family and tradition. I yearned to be lifted into the light like that, surrounded by generations. From the kitchen, several busboys exited with trays of food for the party and I suddenly realized that the downstairs kitchen staff were mostly Black and brown. They looked like people in my neighborhood; they looked like my family, like my mom. If she could see me now, pretending to be some rich little white girl. I suddenly became terribly self-conscious. What if someone recognized me here, dressed like an imposter in my velvet-trimmed dress and too-tight shoes. What if I was found out at home and people knew that I was here with my Jewish grandparents? I heard what people in my neighborhood said about Jews. And now, suddenly, embarrassingly, I felt caught out. I was divided and didn't know which part of myself was the real one. I stepped back into the shadows as the waitstaff passed by, taking no notice of me. Then my grandparents called to me and I quickly slipped away.

★ ★ ★

AFTER a few years, the whipsawing of worlds began to take a toll. I was always trying to figure out where I belonged and what was expected of me. I know now that this was me code-switching. Back then, it was just trying to fit in and be loved. When my grandparents would drop me off after a visit, I would insist that they let me out down the block from my house. My mother's voice in my head told me, *We don't need people all up in our business. They don't need to know nothing.* I made sure that I never mentioned my grandparents when I was in my neighborhood, never talked to my friends about where I went on weekends. They were never overtly anti-Semitic, but there was talk of "Jewish landlords" and "rich assholes," so I learned early on not to call attention to the fact that I was half Jewish. At that point I didn't even know what being Jewish meant to me, or if I even was Jewish. With my grandparents, it was the opposite. Whenever I went out with my grandmother, it was made clear that the slang I used at home was not welcome with them, so I changed up my language and cadence accordingly. I absorbed the negative images white people had around being poor and Black and the ones Black people had around being wealthy and Jewish and I wondered who I was in all of that. And who I wasn't.

When I was ten, a boy around my age moved in next door to my grandparents and we quickly became friends. He was British and his dad was a big executive at a bank, so he moved a lot. Harry was long and lanky and had a mop of blond hair that hung in his face. When he asked if I lived at my grandparents' house I lied and told him I did. I don't know why I did it and, even as I was doing it, I knew it was totally unsustainable. I guess none of my friends at home knew who I was here, and I was curious to find out who that girl was. Harry and I would meet up at our adjoining back gardens or swim in each other's pools. We would hide out in his mother's fur closet, kept cool to suit the sable, eating snacks made by his housekeeper. I donned a cloak of invisibility and slipped, disguised, into his luxurious world.

Untethered from who I was, it was lonelier then I expected it to be. Harry was funny and self-deprecating and we liked each other a lot. But I continued to lie to him, unable to show him who I really was even when I wanted to. When he had to move again several months later, I was desperately happy to see him go, relieved that my lie hadn't been found out. I had already begun to ruthlessly compartmentalize my life according to who I was with: my mother (balance), grandmother (presentable), father (easygoing) and friends (street). It was a moving target. The tensions of balancing social expectations, racism, classism and family history grew stronger over the years as I became more aware of the opportunities I had that my mother and friends didn't. I felt lucky and ashamed. I was old enough to understand the inequality and hostility that the people I loved felt for each other, but too young to do anything about it.

* * *

FAKEER had remained a constant presence in my life over the years. After he left for India, he was gone for about six months, and then he returned so that we could see each other. I was thrilled to have him back, and when my mom worked night shifts at the shelter, I began to stay with him in a small apartment in a communal living arrangement he had with other Sannyasins. He was driving a cab again and saving up to return to India the following year. Now separated, my parents still had an incredibly fraught relationship. As their kid, the contention was complex and difficult to manage. To my mother, words were her warfare and she would disparage my no-account father to me whenever she was given the opportunity. My dad was also antagonistic toward her, and when he would come to pick me up for a night they would inevitably get into a screaming match at the door. From what I could tell, the child support payments were a constant battle and their miscommunication around time management was another. She would expect him at one time and he would arrive hours later, loose and smiling, caught off guard by her fury.

But the real reason for my mother's anger was that she had loved him and he had not loved her back. She had been willing to follow him to the ends of the earth and he had not wanted her. Once, when he had arrived to see me with a female friend in the car, my mother jealously attacked him on the street in front of our apartment, beating at him until he shoved her away and fled. I watched him take off from the living room window, furious at her for chasing him away, and filled with disappointment. After that, I devised a system for when I was supposed to see him. I would stay waiting at the window, ready to move quickly when I would eventually see him turn onto my block, my apprehension and girded hope rewarded with a burst of excitement when he finally showed up. I would grab my bag and run out of the house, getting an insurmountable head start on my mom. My dad would throw open the passenger side door, I would hop in, and we would be gone before they had a chance to fight.

When Fakeer returned to India the following year we had a mainly epistolary relationship, keeping in touch through letters and the occasional crackling, echoing phone call. His letters from the ashram in Pune were always incredibly vivid and riotously drawn. Telling me in detail about his grand spiritual journey and microbial gut issues. He always seemed to have malaria or some amoeba churning up his digestive tract and making him have loose shits. Always brutally honest and searingly open, he would write in the hopes that I could understand why he had to be so far away sometimes. I understood it but still missed him terribly when he was gone in those early days. He seemed to always be on the move, and I would receive envelopes with multiple stamps from Oregon, Nepal, Amsterdam and places farther flung. I held onto these letters religiously when he was gone, like sacred scrolls, reading and rereading them. Tracing my finger over the raised penmanship.

* * *

THE same year that I pretended to live next door to Harry, my mother and I moved into a low-income housing project at Christie and Dupont Streets, close to where the Christie Pits riots my grandfather had witnessed took place. The development was bordered by railroad tracks and a junk-yard where people dumped their garbage. The apartment was small, but clean and cozy, and it was the first place I'd lived that felt like a home. I made neighborhood friends, covered my walls in Michael Jackson posters and wore out *Thriller*, Lionel Richie and the Pointer Sisters on my yellow Sony Walkman. My friends and I would ride in a gang on our banana-seat bikes through our housing complex, a warren of back-alley shortcuts and cement parking lots. Our multicolored tassels fluttering from our handlebars and basketball cards stuck in the spokes. At the corner store we bought handfuls of Fun Dips with their candy stick and packets of flavored powder. Eating them all at once, staining our mouths blue and our tongues red. I wore out my favorite *Fame* T-shirt, bell-bottoms and scuffed Adidas. I cried at the finale of *M*A*S*H* and waited eagerly for every new episode of *The A-Team*, *Knight Rider* and *Fame*. I was Coco, of course. That year my neighborhood friends and I waited in line at the local theater on two-dollar Tuesdays to see movies like *Return of the Jedi, The Outsiders* and *Flashdance*. It was a time of immense freedom for me and huge change in the culture around us.

This was around the same time my grandparents sold their big house and bought a condominium in the Yorkville neighborhood in the heart of downtown Toronto. All of their children were married and out of the house and my grandmother had tired of cleaning and managing such a huge property. Yorkville was a high-end stretch of shopping and entertainment where my grandparents settled into a luxury apartment with a grand entrance and a doorman. Now that they weren't so far north, they were close enough that I could bike to their place and didn't need one of my parents to take me. I would often go after school for a snack and a chat. I remember watching Michael Jackson's "Thriller" video with my grandmother for the first time on one of these visits. We sat mesmerized in front of her large wood-paneled television set, marveling at these new-fangled music videos.

★ ★ ★

THE triumvirate of my mother, grandmother and me had moved into a new phase. I was much more comfortable moving between their worlds now that I was able to get myself around. My mother's long working hours allowed me the freedom to visit my grandmother without my mother's knowledge, but the antipathy between my grandparents and mother remained. It was always just beneath the surface. A simmering resentment that had calcified into their diametrically opposed versions of "what had happened" and "who was right." Although I was beginning to find freedom in other parts of my life, I continued to carry the burden of the relationship between my mother and grandmother.

My mom was still working at the women's shelter and, that summer, she seemed to finally be hitting her stride. We had a good routine going in those days. My mom would pick up a fast-food dinner on the way home and I would have the table set and ready. After dinner, I would do the dishes while my mom would rub her feet and we would talk about our day. Saturday mornings were for cleaning the bathroom and vacuuming the apartment and then, later that day, she worked the night shift. When my dad was out of town, I would sometimes go with her on her overnight shifts and the two of us would bed down in her office. I recall the shelter being a place filled with laughter and tears and loads of kids. Every Saturday night the women would bring what they could to the communal kitchen and everyone would cook together. Women of all backgrounds and cultures and socio-economic situations chopping and frying. A pregnant mother of three with bruises on her face making her Polish pierogies. The old woman who lived in the park across the street stirring a Jamaican stew. The kitchen was always loud and filled with us kids and overlapping conversations in all kinds of languages.

Some nights, angry, drunken exes would come pounding on the door and my mom would grab the shelter's baseball bat that was kept leaning in the corner. She would stand at the padlocked door and talk him down until he left to sleep it off or the cops arrived. My mother seemed strong and capable there and I was proud to be her kid. So it was a surprise when I would sometimes catch her late at night, sitting at our kitchen table, drinking alone. It was not as financially perilous for us anymore—she was working and my dad was mostly paying his child support on time—but she still seemed achingly lonely and needed steadying. When she had been drinking, which had started to become more frequent, she would often take out her anxiety and loneliness on me. It would usually begin after I had been on an overnight visit to my grandparents' apartment or gone with them to the Primrose for dinner. Even though my mother had actively facilitated these visits early on, she had also held on to the bitterness and shame of her early encounters with Phil and Shirley. This unresolved rage would eventually be unleashed in a wave of pent-up anger. "You think you're some rich little white girl now! Let me tell you, you're no better than everybody else. Those people will always think you was nothing. Believe me I know." "I know, Mama."

I had learned to play defense early, and as I got older I just shut down until she got tired of venting. It always made me have second thoughts about my trips to my grandparents', knowing what would be waiting for me when I returned home. When my routine preteen rebellion was taken as disrespect after one of my visits, she wouldn't speak with me for days, furious at my perceived lack of gratitude. Eventually there would be a thaw and we would begin speaking again. I loved my mother, but as I got older I yearned to be out of the pernicious reach of her furious, darkening moods. Heliotropic, I inclined toward the sun.

Chapter Nine

I<small>N 1983, F</small>AKEER HAD RETURNED TO T<small>ORONTO FOR GOOD</small> and wanted me to start living with him part-time. He had become tired of the constant back-and-forth and wanted to have a home where we could live together. He had also come back in part to make amends with Phil and Shirley. Over the years, Shirley had slowly managed to bring the two men back to her dinner table. My father had also found the right balance of medication and meditation as he got older. He had built a tight-knit community of friends and lovers and was more balanced than in his tumultuous early years. He and his father had haltingly begun to repair their fractious relationship, and now that he was settled in Toronto, Fakeer was living off dividends of the family business and the money he made from driving a cab. It was loosely worked out that I would spend my weekends with him, holidays with my grandparents and the week with my mother.

I was thrilled with the idea of having my dad back in my life. I had missed him during his long absences and loved him fiercely. He was always moving apartments and switching roommates, so it was a peripatetic existence whenever I was with him. It was exciting, but also like repeatedly having the rug pulled out from under you. It could be very lonely and sometimes scary when he would be gone for hours in a meditation and I didn't know where he was. It forced me to find my feet and figure out how to navigate a third world, my dad's world.

Fakeer had always been interested in photography, and in my earliest memories of him in Toronto he has at least two cameras strapped over his shoulder wherever we went. We spent our weekends together photographing in downtown parks or in the east end at the beach. While he found the right aperture or reframed a shot I roamed through the trees or collected rocks. We also spent hours in a rented darkroom where he developed the photos from that day's shoot, bathed in red light and the smell of the chemicals sloshing around in white plastic bins. The images revealing themselves slowly at first and then in a rush to judgment. I often went to the Chinese restaurant that was beside the rented darkroom and ordered my favorite greasy egg rolls. I sat there and read for hours while I waited for him to finish. Books became a refuge from loneliness when my dad would disappear into his pictures, so I was a voracious reader. I left oily finger prints on the dog-eared pages of Judy Blume or the Narnia books. I went so often that the kind family who owned the restaurant began to invite me to dinner with their kids in their apartment behind the restaurant.

*　*　*

THOUGH my dad was settled in Toronto, my mom remained suspicious of him. She often picked me up from school and we'd stake out his place to see if he was living high on the hog while making child care payments that she felt were insufficient. Of course, she also wanted to see if he was dating someone new. "Come on, babe, we have to get there in time to get a good parking spot!" she'd yell out the car window as I left the school grounds. We would buy a bucket of Kentucky Fried Chicken, fries, biscuits and a small tub of pink macaroni salad. Then we'd park across the street from his apartment and wait and watch. She'd put the car in park and cut the engine, spreading dinner out on the dashboard and handing me a napkin. I loved those buckets of KFC and would tear into the deep-fried chicken, both of us eating in contented silence.

"What homework do you have tonight?" she'd ask. I'd bring out my books and lay them out on my lap. "English and math." "Alright, well get to it." We would finish up the last of the gravy and fries and my mom would pack up the garbage while I read and completed my homework. As the sun set to night my mom kept watch on my dad's apartment. "Car!" The lights of a car would flash by and we'd scramble and duck to avoid being seen. When it got late, we'd put the seats back and listen to Whitney Houston and Lionel Richie and talk. Snacking on crappy candy my mom had picked up from the bulk store. "This is fun, right, babe?" I would nod. "Sure, Mama."

Although I was pretty certain hiding out in front of your dad's house was not normal behavior, I actually did enjoy our clandestine stakeouts. My mom could be smart and funny, and in those moments, without much else to do, we were able to just enjoy being mother and daughter. Eventually I would fall asleep under a blanket in the back seat. We never caught him at anything, and after a while neither of us really looked that hard. Then one night he spotted us and came storming out of the house. "What in the hell are you doing!?" My mother sat up and quickly started the engine while I waved at my dad. "Puja! What the hell?" My mother lurched into gear and he watched us drive off incredulously. Our stakeouts stopped after that.

* * *

EVERY summer my dad would travel to a Sannyas commune he frequented in the Laurentians, a region of lakes and mountains in Quebec, northwest of Montreal. For my dad, these local Sannyas communes were made up of friends and other disciples of Bhagwan who gathered to share in the master's teachings when they couldn't be in his presence in India. Fakeer would participate in weeks-long meditation groups that were intense and often transformative. Recently, my dad had been traveling between Toronto and Bhagwan's intentional community in Oregon called Rajneeshpuram, or "The Ranch." Bhagwan had recently moved to the United States and had begun to build a religious community in Wasco County, Oregon. The city-sized Rajneeshpuram was to be the center for Bhagwan and his followers in North America. Over the next few years things would go horribly off the rails and the move would turn out to be a legal and political disaster for the movement and for Bhagwan himself. But it was early days and my dad always returned from his trips to Oregon excited and energized by what was happening on the West Coast. But every summer he would return to the commune in Quebec.

The summer I turned twelve, I went with him for the first time. There, we were going to meet up with my dad's friends and fellow Sannyasins for a couple of weeks. I was excited to get out of the city and spend so much uninterrupted time together. But there was also that stone of anxiety in the pit of my stomach. When I was living with Fakeer, he would often vanish and I would find him after a long meditation or waking from a nap. During those times

I would be left to fend for myself. I was now at the age that it was thrilling to be trusted so implicitly, but it could also be very lonely.

"Make sure those crazy white people don't touch you," my mother warned as I finished getting packed. "Those people are funny in the head, you believe me, child. Do not let anyone lay a hand on you." Heading out the door: "I know, Mama!" Fakeer pulled up in his beat-up Volvo station wagon, blaring a discourse by Bhagwan, and we were off. We drove east and north for hours, talking about politics, philosophy and meditation, the cement gray of the city changing to a thick, verdant wall of green. When we finally arrived at the end of a winding dirt road, we saw the community set up beside a sparkling blue lake enclosed by birch and maple trees. As we drove in, several naked people in groups and couples walked by us, chatting casually. They wore sun hats and thick socks with comfortable shoes, a sandal or Birkenstock, and nothing else. I tried not to appear surprised, but watched them retreating in the side-view mirror incredulously. The commune consisted of a few dozen people; some of them lived there permanently but most were just there for the summer and would then move on. We pulled up to a hodgepodge of tents and lodges that had been set up in a semicircle around the lake. Everywhere I looked, there were hippies and Sannyasins dressed in red and orange clothing. Everyone was hirsute, dirty and beautiful. They spoke French and Italian and German, and, as I came to see, meditated freely and danced wildly. These were my father's people, and I felt a free-spirited kinship right away. It was the same feeling I had once sought out at Adventure Playground: an abandonment of social norms and the full-throttle embrace of pagan wildness.

* * *

WE set up in two rooms in an old inn in the woods, wide wooden floorboards with Indian fabrics hanging at the windows. The light from outside painting the walls in washes of marigold and ocean blue. My dad made the antique metal beds with old pillows and throws and quickly settled in for a nap in his room. I lay on my bed listening to the breeze and the sound of laughter and splashing in the water. At dusk we ate a vegetarian meal of chickpeas, lentils and naan in a wide-open field dotted with wildflowers. I loved hearing people passionately discuss politics and philosophy, gesticulating wildly, all tan skin, beaded necklaces and white teeth. That night there was a full-moon party where I was gathered with the women to perform a sacred female ceremony. I watched as the women decorated themselves in mud and beads, their pendulum breasts swinging in the breeze. I shyly wrapped beads and flowers in my sweaty hair and painted my face with two crooked swipes of mud and stayed fully dressed. The gray-haired woman who seemed to be leading us stepped into the center of the circle. "My sisters, now we celebrate and give gratitude to the female spirit by singing and ululating!" The women responded by releasing a loud surge of rooted female energy and noise into the universe. For a kid just coming into my own gender and sexuality, it was electrifying and powerful and horribly embarrassing.

The men, including my father, gathered down near the lake and danced naked or in loin cloths around a bonfire, playing the drums. They grunted and banged their chests, growling and howling up at the moon in their own sacred male ceremony. All pale-blue-veined skin and huge hairy mounds of pubic hair. We women walked down from the field trailing stalks of flowers and the scent of patchouli and joined them in song and wild, gesticulating dance. My dad weaved his way over and grabbed my hands so that we could howl at the moon together as sparks from the fire drifted up toward the inky black night. Whether it was the drums or the night or the fact that no one gave a shit what you did, I finally dropped the cringing preteen attitude and let loose, singing and stomping the ground. Howling in wild, hippie abandon. This was so radically different from my other lives back home with my grandparents and mother. I felt drunk with freedom.

* * *

ONE day, my dad was doing an extended Kundalini meditation and I was exploring the commune on my own, eating an apple. I came upon a young French-Canadian couple making love in their hut in the woods. Curious but embarrassed, I hid behind a tree. They spotted me and told me I could watch if I wanted to. "It's a beautiful thing, man," the woman said, her long brunette hair falling over an alabaster shoulder. The guy nodded. "No hang-ups here ." He smiled a lopsided grin under unruly blond curls. I was pretty sure this was the scenario my mother had warned me against, but I took a spot on a log anyway and watched as they got around to it. The experience was incredibly educational. *So that's how it all works!* I thought. Eventually I finished my apple, got bored and continued on my way.

★ ★ ★

MY dad and I ambled toward the beach one morning near the end of our stay. We didn't have much of an agenda; he was going to sign up for an afternoon group and then we were going for a swim in the lake. The beach was clothing optional, but everybody opted to be nude. I, on the other hand, was steadfastly wearing my one-piece bathing suit and had a towel wrapped under my armpits. I was not ready to be naked around my naked father, no matter how cool the beach vibe was. My dad wasn't wearing anything except a bright orange sarong around his waist and a large sun hat. He was extolling the virtue of a radically atheistic life over his quasi-religious upbringing. "My father's the poster boy for religious appearances over radical acceptance and the loss of ego. It's all ego with my folks. He's been on the board of every synagogue we've ever belonged to and I don't think I've ever had a discussion with him about God or higher purpose. It was just business and success with him, that's what he worshipped. They left me to fend for myself in the moral wilderness!"

We reached the beach and I stopped, the brilliant blue of the lake sparkling between stands of thick spruce trees. "You left me too ," I said. I didn't know I was going to say it, right up until the moment the words left my mouth. But when I finally said them, I realized I had been wanting to speak those words for a long time. Many times, I had formed them in my mouth and rolled them across my tongue like a pebble. My dad sat down on the beach beside me. "What's that, Puja?"

I took a deep breath. "I know that you didn't want me. My mom told me lots of times that you wanted her to have an abortion." He took a deep breath and I could tell I had landed my punch.

"When I first heard your mom was pregnant, you're right, I wasn't ready to be anyone's dad."

My heart raced and my hands shook. "Then why did you bother?"

He took a minute and then answered. "Because once I held you and met you, I loved you."

I shook my head. "Then why did you leave me? When

you moved out. You left me with my mom and she wasn't doing good."

My dad nodded, a sad look coming over his face. "You're right. I did. It was such a traumatic time for me and I didn't know what else to do. But you're right. I did leave your mom, and you."

Tears welled up in my eyes. "I've been so afraid to tell you how hard it was. 'Cause I thought you'd get mad and leave again. And this time you might not come back." I was gulping back tears. "She was so sad and I didn't know how to make her better. And I missed you so much."

Now my dad and I were both crying. "I'm so sorry you got hurt, Pooj." He let the apology hang in the air, unadorned and bare-faced. He didn't try and gussy it up with excuses and obfuscations to justify his actions. Just a quiet recognition of the pain and sadness he had caused. He took my hand while I cried and we sat in silence looking out over the water. My tears eventually dried up and I realized that some secret little compartment in which I had kept the pain of my dad's leaving had unlocked. "Okay. I just wanted to tell you." And just like that it lifted.

My dad smiled. "You ready for a swim?" I stood up resolutely and asked my dad to hold my towel. He held it up and I hid out of view behind it. I then stripped my one-piece bathing suit to my ankles and kicked it away. With a terrified whoop I sprinted naked across the sand and into the lake in a spray. My body swallowed up by the bracingly cold water, unfettered and free. I came to the surface with a cry of delight.

* * *

TRIPS to the commune became a regular part of my summers with my dad. I remember them as exciting, beautiful and sometimes lonely. When we were together, my dad was a thrilling iconoclast, railing against conformity. He led me to intellectual revolution and encouraged free thought. His community was a third world that I inhabited, a place I could try on my burgeoning sexuality and burning intellectual curiosity. It was a place to seek, ask questions and celebrate the spiritual. I began to enthusiastically participate in discussions at dinner, the sun setting golden over a table of vegetables, homemade bread and jams. Skinny-dip in the lake under the hot full sun. Dance to drums as if no one was watching. Then, as quickly as those summers had begun, he would have to leave in the fall: for Oregon again, or an adventure in the Himalayas, for some pretty little Sannyasin he had met in Europe. I would return to the city and remember him and our time together at the commune as if it were a fever dream.

Chapter Ten

IN THE FALL OF 1983, WHEN I WAS TEN YEARS OLD, MY mom was out one night at a backyard barbecue and she met a tall, affable white guy named Dave. She liked that Dave was unflappable and deeply decent and he liked her warm eyes and smile. They quickly fell in love. Dave was a country boy in the city; kind, curious and smart, he had been brought up in the small, rural farming town of Omemee, Ontario, a conservative, white, protestant bastion. Dave's parents, Doug and Bev, Omemee's postmaster and a homemaker, brought their two boys up in a loving and conservative home. After Dave moved to the city for school, he worked as a computer programmer and wore plaid dress shirts, toques and large square glasses. He had a long, lean, horsey look and easy gait that I liked immediately. He seemed a safe harbor in the storm, a solid adult we could count on.

Within the year we were living with Dave in a small house on Winona Drive and my mom was pregnant. From what I could tell she had quit drinking, and to my relief, my visits with my grandparents became far less contentious. She was happy with Dave, assured in his love of her, and we were a solid family. Winona Drive was a quiet, tree-lined street in the west end of the city, and we had a backyard with a small garden. The house was full of Dave and my mom's friends and their kids. My mom had made friends through her work at the shelter and we were now part of a multicultural mix of families. Unlike in California, where she had felt like an outsider, she was now part of a tight-knit community where she and Dave were not the only mixed-race couple. This community was a welcome change from the intense claustrophobic connection that had always been the norm between my mother and me. Dave introduced us to a Toronto filled with small out-of-the-way restaurants serving dahl in Kensington Market, simmering bulgogi in Little Korea and chicken tikka masala out on Gerrard East. We wore matching toques knitted by Bev and he walked me to school before work every morning. When my mom went into labor just a few days before Christmas I sat in the front seat of the ambulance as Dave nervously held my mom's hand in the back. The ambulance driver turned on the lights and siren to give me a thrill and I shrieked out loud laughing. When my sister was born several hours later, Dave brought me into the room and I was allowed to hold the baby. I immediately fell in love with Lea. She was a gorgeous baby with huge brown eyes and pudgy little fists. I had been an only child for so many years and now I finally had a sister. An equal and someone with whom I could share my days. Once we were home, I carried her everywhere, refusing to put her down even when she slept. She, more than Dave or the crowded, sweet little house on Winona, made us feel like a fully formed family. She would be my comrade in arms.

* * *

WHEN Lea was six months old, I was told we were moving out of Toronto to start a new life together. Dave had been talking for a while about living in the country, something closer to how he grew up. Although my mom seemed less enthusiastic about leaving the city, she eventually bought into his dream. When he got a job in Fredericton, New Brunswick, an east coast town of fifty thousand people, they decided to move. I had a last visit with my grandmother and we hugged a lot more than usual and promised to write each other. She was not usually one to show much emotion, but as I hopped out of her car I could tell she was holding back tears. It was most difficult to say goodbye to my dad, and I cried mightily the last time I saw him in Toronto. Then all of our belongings were packed into a U-Haul trailer and hitched behind Dave's yellow Volkswagen Rabbit, and we traveled east.

We drove to Montreal, down through New York state, across Maine and eventually into New Brunswick. We then drove up the beautiful salt-sprayed coast to Fredericton. It took us three days to get there and my sister and I spent the trip rolling around in the backseat in a makeshift bed of blankets and pillows while watching the country flicker by. In Fredericton, Dave and Jean had rented a big old Victorian in the center of town for six months. The plan was to live in town while my mom and Dave looked for a house in the country and he started work at a computer programming firm. A rope swing hung from a massive northern red oak as we pulled in tired and hot. The home belonged to a professor on sabbatical. He and his wife and their five children had left to travel in Southeast Asia for a year. The house was like something out of a fairy tale, broken down and magical. A six-bedroom maze of rooms, small back stairways and hidden nooks. The living room was filled with furniture covered in thick corduroy material and on the wide wood-plank floors lay colorful Moroccan rugs. The hallway upstairs was long and wide and the bedrooms off of it were cluttered and filled with toys and maps and dreams of kids I would never meet. I spent the first few months we lived there discovering worlds within those upstairs rooms. Pirates on the high seas, astronauts floating in deep space. I explored for hours with my sister on my hip. I dressed her up from a basket of well-made Swedish doll's clothes that I had found in a cupboard and we roamed from room to room. Books were everywhere, piled in the closets and stacked on their shelves. Lea and I could often be found tucked away in a back bedroom where I would read endless Judy Blume and anything by Madeleine L'Engle to her.

Even though it was exciting, it was also bewildering at first, and my mom worried to Dave about being one of only a few Black people in town. A few weeks in, my mother and I were grocery shopping and she became irate when a security guard began to follow us, the only people of color in the store. "You need to back up off of us!" she hissed as she grabbed my hand roughly, leaving our cart and walking out. As a newly arrived Black woman in a small, very white town, she felt the glances and slights keenly.

★ ★ ★

THE kitchen was the center of our home, a wide-open room with a large country table and wrap-around wooden benches where we would play board games and cribbage. The cupboards were painted lime green and the walls sky blue, and the professor and his family had hung Hundertwasser prints and crocheted wall hangings. We started sprouting beans and keeping wild rice and granola in tins on the Formica counter. My mom washed and

I dried the dishes in front of a window that opened onto a shambolic garden in the back where mint and basil grew alongside wild roses and black-eyed Susans.

Dave cooked dinner most nights as my sister and I listened to Joni Mitchell and Frank Zappa on a record player in the corner. We were happy and content as the weather cooled and summer quickly turned to fall.

I started fourth grade at a small elementary school just a few blocks away from the house on a tree-lined street. I was nervous about being a new brown city kid meeting small-town white kids. But the kids were kind if somewhat confused by our mixed family and unconventional parentage. I made friends with a couple of girls who had bowl cuts and ruddy cheeks and also lived close to the school. We would walk home after class, stopping at each other's homes for snacks and cookies and chocolate milk. They were solidly white, middle-class families where the dads worked outside the house and the mothers looked after the kids. It was so strange to me that I found it fascinating, this world of nuclear families I had only imagined from books.

As the fall made its inexorable march toward winter, the leaves blazed burnished red, gold and yellow. My friends and I walked home as the leaves twisted and turned in the wind, searching out the sidewalk below. Fredericton had a tree canopy that was dense and varied, and the streets and backyards we cut through were filled with hundreds of varieties like white pine, eastern hemlock and northern red oak.

Our treasured brown Klondike boots made a double-lined trench as we walked through the thick blanket of fallen, rustling color. The frigid North Atlantic wind blowing in off the Bay of Fundy and curving down the Saint John River made it hard to breath. It came in violent gusts and gales and hunched our shoulders to the slate gray sky. The East Coast Atlantic air carrying the smell of salt, fish and lands beyond our imagination. Our winter coats already drawn against its icy mood and temperament.

* * *

My mom had started making bean soups from scratch and baking seeded bread, and the scent would greet me after school as I flung open the door and threw my knapsack and coat in the corner. My sister squealing at me from her high chair, face covered in mashed squash or pureed peas. I would tell my mom about my day and she would listen distractedly as she washed the dishes staring out the window. After what felt like an auspicious beginning, I could tell she had not settled in as well as the rest of us, and she seemed restless. She hadn't made many friends and kept to herself after overhearing a few ignorant comments and out of a fear of being singled out. Her isolation only grew as Dave started work and she was left alone all day in the rambling house with my baby sister. She was struggling without her work or a community to turn to for support. Once again, I took it upon myself to try to cheer her with funny stories from school and tales from the neighbors. She would try to listen, watching the coming storms through our kitchen window with trepidation and a loose, unfixed melancholy.

Winter came hard and fast that year, dumping snow that relentlessly blew in from the St. Lawrence. Dave and my mom finally bought a house outside of town and we packed up again and moved to the country. I would be attending a smaller country school and had to leave the "downtown" schoolhouse. I was sad to leave my friends and the new house lacked the magic of our first. Instead, it was a solid three-bedroom bungalow built in the seventies. It stood at the end of a long driveway, and we had to park at the bottom until Dave could figure out a way to clear it. The snow in that part of the country fell thick and deep and went on as far as the eye could see. Off the front porch, you were easily in up to your chin where the snow had piled up the side of the house. The air was bitterly cold and clear and the sky a crystal blue when it wasn't dumping freezing rain or big, tumbling snowflakes. With the snow and the ice and the move came a silence I had never experienced. Out in the country, in deep winter, it was so silent we could hear a car driving by a field away. I could hear my mom and Dave fighting in whispered tones behind their closed door at night. She hated it out here by herself when Dave commuted into town for work. She was lonely without her community to fall back on and Dave was frustrated that she hadn't given it a chance. I had started school but hadn't made any friends yet. I hated the long yellow-school-bus ride where I sat by myself, motion sick and anxious. I was glad when the holiday break finally came.

That Christmas, Lea and I got matching thick blue flannel pajamas and red knitted slippers from Bev. I received a large wooden dollhouse that was stocked with wooden furniture, small, woven rugs and tiny plants made of felt. My mom had ordered a pint-sized wooden Black family that I loved and who immediately moved in and lived there quite comfortably. I spent hours arranging and rearranging the people, making the beds, placing the television and couches and hanging hand-drawn pictures on the wallpapered walls. After the holidays, as things quickly seemed to grow colder between my mom and Dave, I focused on that dollhouse and the family I could control.

* * *

THAT was the winter I began to dream of fire. Every night as the days grew brutally short and the nights long, I dreamt of fire spreading through our home. Flames greedily catching the rug and ferociously climbing the walls. I dreamt that the hallway outside my room quickly turned into a raging conflagration blocking every path out. My sister crying out to be saved as I would wake up screaming. My mom or Dave would come quickly to my bedside and try to calm me. Assuring me that I was okay and the dreams weren't real. But once they began, the dreams came regularly, always terrifying and grotesquely predictable. No one survived. I started to sleep on the floor next to my sister's crib so that I could save her if the fire came for us. I planned escape routes and left the window in our room cracked open so that we could jump out and into the snow drift below. I drew up secret plans on paper to save my family, earnestly measuring the length of the hallway and mapping it out. Doing test runs and timing them on my Casio watch to see how long it took to get to my mom and Dave's room from my own. Dave and my mom eventually tired of dissuading me and let me sleep where I wanted and measure what I needed to. It was exhausting, but I had to remain vigilant and awake, always awake, head snapping erect as I tried in vain to keep ahead of the flames. But as night descended and the snowstorms raged outside, the fire always came.

* * *

THE first sign of spring was the fog rolling in off the Saint John River. A thick, damp creeping fog that would chum and wisp the frozen shores of the river and then crawl across the forest below. The thick tumble of sea rolling right up the hill to the house. It was so dense that I could watch its slow progression up our lawn in the cold early-morning light. Eventually the sun would rise above the tree line and burn it off in wisps. The ice and snow had finally started to give way. In our backyard, the fiddleheads, thick and electric green, began unfurling and poking their way through the sodden blanket of fallen leaves. On one of these spring mornings Dave told my mother he was unhappy, had been for a while, and was leaving her. I came home from school and found her weeping in the bathroom, devastated and furious. I could feel how out of control she was and immediately felt that our world had shifted. I shut myself in my room while she raged and lashed out at him through the night. I cradled my sister in my bed while she slept, scared and crying. It immediately reminded me of my mom and dad fighting years ago. The next morning Dave packed up a few bags and moved out. He quietly knocked on my door before he left but I didn't answer. I could hear him standing in the hall, shuffling his feet. As if he was stalling, trying to figure out a way forward.

After Dave moved out my mom slowly started to slide into another depression. She quickly packed me up and I was sent back to Toronto to stay with my dad. I was shipped off before the end of the school year and left with only a small suitcase and my tiny Black dollhouse family. Dave was staying in town until they could sell the house and then they would both get apartments back in Toronto. I flew back and never got the chance to say goodbye to anyone. I remember that the flight was the first time I had flown by myself on an airplane. The stewardesses were so glamorous in their uniforms and they were incredibly kind. The plane wasn't full so they sat with me and gossiped and we drank soda. My mom never let me have soda, too much sugar. At the end of the flight they also gave me a whole bag of the plane's mints.

Dave eventually took Lea when the house in New Brunswick was sold so my mom could look for an apartment in Toronto. It was devastating to have my sister living with Dave while I lived with my dad. I had drawn up routes, made plans and promised to protect her and now she too was beyond my reach. While it was a relief to be in my dad's wild, affectionate presence again after such a heavy winter, I still ached for Dave and missed my sister terribly. Dave had been a steady presence and a ballast for us. With him gone, my mother became untethered and utterly misanthropic. He had proven all of her worst misgivings about the world and men. No one was to be trusted and no dream relied on. Our fragile family had lasted a little over two years. In the end the fire had crept down the hall and come for us after all. Burning up our family and leaving nothing but ash.

Chapter Eleven

MY MOTHER WAS ABLE TO SECURE A RENTAL IN the same low-income housing project that we had lived in years earlier near Christie Pits. She applied for a small three-bedroom townhouse and we moved in within weeks. Dave and my mom shared joint custody of my sister, so she spent half of the week living with him while I was back to living part-time with my dad. He and I would often visit Shirley together to have a swim in the pool or eat lunch. Returning to my dad and grand-mother quickly helped settle me back into a routine in Toronto. Having missed the end of the school year, moved homes and lost Dave, I was looking for some stability. My mother was still heartbroken and deeply resentful of Dave, but she had managed to get something together back in the city. She got her job back at the shelter, and having a community of women around her again was a necessary support. But we were both still raw and haltingly figuring out how to put our life back together. That summer, my mom decided we would go spend a few weeks with her family in Ohio while my sister was with Dave.

My mother and I returned to Ohio over the Fourth of July holiday to stay with our huge family there. We arrived at the Dayton airport, carrying bags of cheap gifts clutched in my mother's ringed fingers. Shabby Christmas decor was still strung through the airport in random places: ropes of tinsel hanging from the banisters, a battered plastic Santa tilting in a corner next to the bathroom. My mother's twin sister, Aunt Joann, was there to meet us. Jean and Joann, were still radically opposite in personality and demeanor but an almost exact physical replica of each other. Sometimes one or the other was a little heavier, or one had her hair in a short Afro while the other had hers hot-combed straight. But to the untrained eye, there was almost no telling them apart. The differences were only under the surface, where my mom was quiet and withdrawn while my aunt Joann was still rowdy and full of chutzpah. I would spend the trip watching my aunt talk and laugh, her warm brown eyes tracing back and forth to my mom and then to me. They shared high cheekbones and crooked teeth in wide, goofy smiles. The whole family, back to Alonzo, has arcus senilis corneae, a benign eye condition that has the haunting effect of creating a liquid blue ring around dark black pupils. It was another trait the twin sisters shared. Aunt Joann had three daughters by three different men and worked two jobs to support them. She was amazing, funny and, even though she must have been exhausted, always ready to party.

Joann's three daughters, my wonderful and wild cousins, Jean-Jean, Julli and Jollina, did not look anything alike. They were tall and short, round and lean, brown and Black and tan, but each was entirely feisty and street smart. Jean-Jean, named after my mom—twice—was the oldest. She was caramel-complexioned, built curvy, and sassy as hell. Julli was a couple of years older than me and a wild, rebellious beauty who tested her mother. Jollina was the youngest, wiry and kind, more vulnerable.

As I got older, whenever we went to Ohio we stayed with my Aunt Joann and my three girl cousins. The girls and I slept in the same bedroom together in their small apartment. Joann had moved to Chillicothe, Ohio—a small town on a back-country highway with only a few roads and fewer trees, an hour south of Dayton. In town everyone lived in a baked grid with square lawns and gray siding. Her apartment was on the second floor of a square, nondescript two-story house that looked onto a dusty side road. The four of us girls would lay sprawled in the heat on two beds pushed together in the center of the room. A shag rug on top of wide, worn floorboards and several layers of wallpaper peeling away from the wall. Faded hand-painted flowers holding up stamped orange stripes behind a cowboy print with horses in a lathered gallop. Together my cousins and I were every shade: honey-caramel, dark brown with a high yellow tone, light brown with an olive tinge, and a beautiful deep, dark black. The four of us were daughters of identical twins and four different fathers; we were a genetic crap shoot. Limbs thrown across each other, the heat melting us into a dark, bored teenage tan.

One afternoon during an annual visit, a group of boys pulled up on their bikes outside, maybe two or three of them with wide smiles and cornrows. I got up and went to the window and opened it. Julli was sweet on one of them and he called out for her. "Hey, Jules! You gonna come on down?" All the girls crowded to the window, jostling for space and calling down to them. "It's too damn hot. We're gonna sweat our hair out!" He winked. "Come on. You can double with me." We grabbed our things and together we rolled out with the group of boys and a crowd of our cousins on ten-speed bikes, cruising through the neighborhood streets. My cousin Chopper had roped a radio to his bike and Radio Cincinnati blasted from the tinny speakers. At the corner store we stopped to get a handful of Freezies, sucking them back until the last of the colored ice had drained, tongues turning a flaming red or antifreeze blue, the sides of our mouths cut from the sharp edge of the plastic. It was a wonderful shock to be surrounded by huge, kinetic groups of cousins and aunts and uncles. It was thrilling to lean into my mother's clan and my Black and brown community. It felt worlds away from the commune in Quebec, the Bridle Path, and even how my mom, sister and I lived in Toronto. Here the Walkers were intensely devoted to their huge, extended family, and being my mother's child immediately granted me familial belonging in a way I had never felt. There was no pressure to code switch. I was welcomed, loudly and proudly, with very little effort on my behalf. I was "Jeanie's oldest" and that was enough. The Walkers were ride or die.

★ ★ ★

THE farmhouse had been sold years earlier, after Doreen's and Alonzo's passing, and was not the family base anymore. Several of the sisters and their children were now settled in and around the same low-income housing project in Dayton, the apartments stacked one on top of the other and the life of the neighborhood spilling out onto the crumbling stoops and the street. Ma Dears hung laundry across their small, dry yards while grandbabies played at their feet on the cracked cement sidewalk. Some had optimistically planted thorny roses that struggled for supremacy under the ceaseless and careless feet of the neighborhood kids.

My aunt Bernice had a hair salon in her apartment on the first floor of the complex. Aunt Bernice was a decade older than my mother and had been her sister/mother when they were growing up. She had taken the twins on as her charges when they were young and now had a fraught relationship with them. They feared her like a strict mother but hated when she transgressed her sisterly role. This happened often, as Aunt Bernice was bossy and demanding with the twins. My Aunt Joann always the first to rebel. "Bernice, you better back off! You don't own me woman. And you ain't Mama." Aunt Bernice would suck her teeth in reproach. While their hair set, the ladies at Aunt Bernice's salon would sit out front wearing plastic capes, gossiping and smoking. Inside the ground floor apartment several hot irons were wielded quick and scolding, the hair giving up the ghost before the Friday night block party. At the end of every grinding, exhausting, scrambling week there was a block party and the whole project would come out. Lights hung across the street and beer and wine coolers sat in ice buckets. Kids ran with sparklers as the adults danced to Kool & the Gang, Al Jarreau and the Commodores. My cousin Julli, the most rebellious of Aunt Joann's three girls, would surreptitiously make out with a neighborhood white boy against a back chain-link fence. My cousins and their friends all crowded in the middle of the street, which had become a dance floor. Hips swaying, arms sinewy with muscle, long limbs and high butts in cut-off jean shorts, dancing in a sweaty exultant scrum. My mom and I held hands and danced together on my aunt Kathleen's stoop under the streetlight. Aunt Kathleen was the most beautiful and terrifying of all the aunts. She had green eyes and a luminous face. She also had a full set of upper dentures that she would remove and drop into your drink when you weren't looking. Aunt Kathleen had a death stare that could catch you from across the room and hold you fast. Those emerald eyes daring you to keep causing a ruckus and make her get up out of her chair. My aunt Kathleen was pure, coiled violence, and you sure as hell never crossed her.

There were several aunts and uncles whom I feared. I would be playing with a cousin and we would get too loud or knock into something and suddenly my cousin would be grabbed and pulled away across the floor. The other kids would instinctively scatter, knowing what was coming, but at first I was so shocked I didn't move. My aunt or uncle, so full of humor and kindness to me, was suddenly dragging their child into another room and locking the door while I stood rooted to the spot. The sound of my cousin being beaten was dull and terrifying. I could hear the belt or fist landing on flesh, bodies flailing and slipping, things being knocked to the ground. The belt on flesh again, followed by loud screams and a begging for it to stop. I soon realized that none of the adults would stop what was happening. They would shush the younger kids and send them outside, waiting for it to pass. Everyone would grow silent, bearing witness to the physical abuse they had endured their whole lives and would now pass down to their children. It was once explained to me by my mother that a Black child was physically disciplined by their parent so they could survive in the violent, wider white world. That some of my aunts and uncles beat their children so that white society would not do worse. An act of love then. But it sure didn't feel that way.

★ ★ ★

EACH Fourth of July, there was a family reunion in a Dayton public park. With fifteen children in my mother's family and their children and grandchildren, the numbers rose into the hundreds. Uncle Thomas was always in charge of the barbecuing. Pounds of pork, chicken and ribs were managed over open flames. He was a big man, but full of energy and light on his feet. There were three or four barbecues that Uncle Thomas somehow managed to transport from various backyards, set up and then man the entire day. While he cooked, he always had a warm smile and jocular charm. The circle of light blue around his black pupils was the most startling in the family. It was an aquamarine ring of fire that had a beauty that was almost hard to look at. He was also morbidly obese and had a slight stutter that turned into a self-conscious laugh. His arm had been broken when the birth women pulled him out of my grandmother's womb and it had never healed properly. It had grown smaller than his other arm and the hand hung limp at the wrist. He cradled it reflexively, like a broken songbird wing, using his good appendage to wield the spatula and tongs at a fervid pace.

Thomas was the twelfth of fifteen births and came right before my mom and Aunt Joann. He, the twins and the baby of the family, Martin, had all remained close over the years and I felt most comfortable around them. They were a full generation younger than their oldest siblings and were less religious and more easy going. Uncle Thomas was married to his grade-school love, an obese white woman who was incredibly sweet but painfully shy about her weight. She also had a big honking laugh when you said something that she found funny, but otherwise didn't talk much except to her husband in a quiet susurration. They had two kids, a boy and a girl; their daughter was short and big like her mama and had long wavy blond hair, alabaster white skin and light blue eyes. Her brother was a tall rangy kid who had tight black curly hair, dark brown skin and deep brown eyes like his father. Uncle Thomas considered himself a lucky man. He had a broken wing that ached in the summer rain, a white daughter, a Black son and a woman he had loved for most of his life.

At events like these, even the vegetables had meat: mashed potatoes with pork gravy, collard greens with ground beef. The varieties of potato salad were legion; every aunt had her own recipe and would bring serving bowls full of the stuff. The pies, oh the pies. My aunt Judy was as lean and vicious as a mad fox but she was an incredible baker. She had lost most of her teeth and was struggling with a heavy alcohol addiction, but get her in a kitchen on a Sunday morning and she had a gift for making beautiful pies. Every conceivable fruit was enlisted: peaches, apples, rhubarb and the stone fruits she'd pick from her apartment's backyard. The fruit was boiled in large dented pots and then mixed with an unholy amount of refined white sugar. The sugar was poured out of an industrial-sized blue-and-red striped bag that she had me sift into a bowl. The two of us laughing while she talked a blue streak. For the crust, she used buckets full of lard and flour and kneaded them into a golden brown dough as if in divination, her thin, wracked body swaying and pushing in a rhythm. The fruit and sugar would then be layered into the pie pan and covered in a crisscross pattern of thick slices of cooled dough. The whole morning her small apartment and the rough hallway outside were filled with the beautiful scent of those cooling golden-crusted pies. The rest of the Fourth of July, Aunt Judy would spend drunkenly fighting her siblings, swearing and dancing until she blacked out in a corner of the park. Someone would eventually put a pillow under her head and cover her with a blanket.

Cars that had been pulled up on the grass pulsed music out of their open doors, and the laughter was constant. Everyone was broke and struggling to get from paycheck to paycheck, but somehow that made it more bearable— we weren't alone. I never spoke with my cousins about the burdens we all carried, financially and emotionally; we just accepted that was the way it was and moved on. Plates balanced on knees while everyone ate on lawn chairs set up in circles. The conversation turned to an incident that had happened years ago. My mother had been a late bloomer with boys, but in her senior year in high school she had a boyfriend and he was her first real love. Tall and gangly, he had big ears and a bright mind. He was the first boy to see my mother's intellect and get excited about it. The two had begun a fumbling intimacy that was physically modest but emotionally expansive. My aunt Rose, slightly older and more sexually advanced, had casually begun an affair with the younger man. Aunt Rose was a tiny fire-cracker and at nineteen was already married to my uncle Par, a tall, dashing ladies' man who served in the air force. Uncle Par's gray-blue Wright-Patterson air force uniform was always cut beautifully on his tall frame, crisp and commanding. He had a perfectly round Afro and a neatly trimmed mustache that always had a sly grin underneath. He drove a cool car and had an easy humor about him, but he was also incredibly promiscuous and controlling. Whether it was to get back at her philandering husband or boredom or both, Aunt Rose took up with my mother's inexperienced boyfriend.

One morning, Par returned from the base early and found his wife and the younger man, naked and asleep in their bed. All hell broke loose and Par ended up pulling out a small pistol he kept in the closet and shooting the young man in the stomach. The man survived, and eventually everyone agreed to go their separate ways without pressing charges. This story was legend in my family and had everyone at the barbecue in stitches—everyone except for my mom and my aunt Rose, who looked over at her sister warily. My mother sat blank-faced and I remember being confused at the casual mention of such violence and betrayal coupled with laughter. The hoary tale told, the laughter died down and eventually the games and basketball started up. My mom got up and walked away silently and Aunt Rose and I watched her go. The sun set to an indigo purple as the streetlights came on and eventually everyone packed up, collected Aunt Judy and made their way home.

* * *

My mother had always been adamant that I should know this side of my family and not just the "rich Jewish side." She hated that I was spending so much time with my grandmother and felt it was encouraging me to "act white." I didn't know what that meant exactly but I knew it wasn't good. In Toronto, she always said she wanted us to be around her family more, but when we were with them, I could tell she didn't feel entirely comfortable. She laughed and joked more than I had ever seen before, but I could also feel her internal anxiety when she was in the rough-and-tumble of it all. I noticed she seemed to want to get away from her family, whereas I craved being in the tumult of so many family members and loved the feeling of a large tribe. Aware of not wanting to "act white," I leaned into being just like my Black relatives.

★ ★ ★

"MAMA, I'm going for a drive with the cousins!"

When we were staying in Dayton, my mom would sometimes let me cruise around with my older cousins in the back seat of their beat-up ride. "Home by dinner!" I blew out the screen door and hopped in the waiting car. We passed boarded-up houses and strip malls, decaying and brown like rotten teeth in a crooked smile. Public Enemy and N.W.A. blared into the stifling heat as my cousins called out to friends who walked by. We saw young men slapping down dominos, fades shaved into the sides of their heads and ropes of gold slung around their necks. Their treasured kicks wiped clean with the rag in their back pocket and vinegar from their mama's cupboard. We passed young girls skipping double Dutch on the sidewalk, stiff pigtails bouncing in unison. Huge plastic baubles, red and pink and attached to the elastics securing their braids tight to their scalps. Their clatter and jump a crowning cacophony. Their feet skipped and moved in unison over the blur of the plastic jump rope; stumbling they laughed, hands covering their wide smiles. We honked at the old-timers, waving from under their striped umbrellas. On the outskirts of town, the boys stopped to take a piss and stretch their lanky legs. Dusk settling all around us, they wrestled and rough-housed, yelping into the slanting light. As we walked through the tall grasses, I braided crowns out of dandelions and placed them on my cousins' heads. They looked like figures in a Basquiat painting: rough innocence full of joy and some unnamable sorrow.

On one drive home it began to rain, lightly at first so that we turned on the windshield wipers and then in a torrent of water the wipers couldn't possibly clear. We drove under a bridge and were quickly submerged in a deep pool of water that had gathered there and rapidly rose to the top of the wheel wells. The engine let out a guttural wheeze and then died, drowning in the murky brown runoff draining to the lowest point. In a panic we all scrambled out of the open windows and to the top of the car roof that had suddenly become an island. Stunned and silent, we listened as the water pounded the overpass above us and continued to rise around us. It poured in the open car windows in a deluge and then filled the empty interior and continued up to the top of the car doors. Somehow the tape deck inside was still working, and Roberta Flack warbled from under the rising water. We huddled together and listened to the sudden and gale-force winds blowing around us. All wide-eyed and shivering in tube tops and cut-off shorts, feeling trapped and cold and scared. My older cousin anxiously talked about trying to swim to safety, but most of my cousins didn't know how to swim and the thought of plunging into that fast-moving, oily water was terrifying. And then, as quickly as it came, the rain let up and the sun that had been hidden behind the twisting black clouds threw out its last beams of surprisingly warm orange and glittering gold. The rushing rivulets eased and the water slowly stopped rising, and then began to retreat. Quickly, as if embarrassed at the indignity of having to slink away. No one moved. We sat silently on our car roof island beneath the underpass. Like some urban tropical natural disaster postcard. Wish you were here. We later found out a tornado had blown through just to the north of Dayton, taking off roofs and tearing up trees by the roots.

★ ★ ★

SUNDAY mornings, my older religious aunts would hustle up as many of us kids as they could and march us over to the tiny red-brick church in downtown Dayton. It occupied its own little square of neatly mowed lawn and the outside was nondescript, neither big enough nor small enough to notice. Clusters of well-kept partridgeberry bushes at its nape, a leaning bell tower pitched out of the roof. Its iron bell sitting slightly askew, the rope hanging down to a hook in the lobby by the coat room. The nave was small and covered in wood, the bottom in vertical planks and the ceiling in wide sheets of plywood. The wood had been cut and processed at a local sawmill over near Xenia way and the smell of pulp lingered in the air on humid days. A worn maroon industrial rug covered the center aisle, and fans in the corners tried to beat back the early morning heat. The only concession to aesthetics was a large framed portrait of a white Jesus hanging between the windows that looked out onto the gravel parking lot.

Once inside, the Walkers would file in jostling and shushing and take up the back two pews. All of us settling in boisterously, my aunties' hands reaching for bibles and smacking the younger boys upside the head with the same motion. On Sunday the older women in church wore hats that matched their dresses and shoes. A pale pelican pink or robin's egg blue from hat to heels, feathers and brims carefully pulled over shiny wigs. We were all women and children except for my uncle Martin, who had been born right after the twins. Martin was the youngest of the siblings and a wild child who was twenty years younger than his older brothers and sisters. To us kids he felt less like an uncle and more like one of us. He was a hilarious raconteur and once in his cups would keep us entertained with his hugely inappropriate humor and wise-cracking ways. He loved to drink and party, and the women in his small sphere of Ohio loved him. For some reason, even with a hangover, a half-drunk girl on his arm or rumpled clothes that his older sisters cut their eyes at, he usually showed up for church. He would come in late, shoving the kids aside until we made room for him to slouch in the pew at the opposite end from his sisters. When the choir began he would take up singing in a raspy, enthusiastic tenor. On stage, the Reverend Jackson stepped into view from the chapel and everyone rose to their feet to continue along with the choir and Uncle Martin singing "How High Art Thy God."

It was always strange to see my mother dressed up with a bible in her hand. At home she railed against the patriarchy of religion, having studied some theology at Antioch, and her experience working at the women's shelter informed her boots-on-the-ground feminism. She enjoyed nothing more than slapping down a high-handed, misogynistic religious proclamation. Even at her lowest she considered herself an intellectual and above blind adherence to the male-dominated religion of her childhood. But here, back in Ohio, she seemed to have decided it was better to just get along, and not to stand out any more than we already did. She had left her small town and large family, desperate for an education but also thrilled to abandon the entrenched ignorance and abuse. Along the way she had burned bridges with some of her siblings who thought she was "too good" and "uppity." When she got pregnant and had to come crawling back, several of my church-going aunts reveled in her come-uppance. And over the years she had kept up appearances to avoid confrontation with her older, more pious sisters. It seemed they had enough to fight about without my mother throwing their white Jesus in their face. She and I stood beside each other and began to sing loudly and with vigor, my mom shooting me a wry glance. Eventually, the piano kicked in and the Reverend Jackson brought my cousin Tammy forward. She was a big girl with a booming, powerful voice and she got that nondescript little church in the center of town rocking.

* * *

AND then, inevitably, at the end of every trip to Ohio we would return to our lives in Toronto. Changed by our time and experiences there. Being with our family provided a ballast for my mom during some rough stretches and became a touchstone that we both returned to. But as much as my mom needed her time there, I could tell she was always happy to leave and we always returned home. When I asked her why, she said, "I built a life in Toronto. It wasn't much maybe, but it was mine and I didn't want to give that up." For me, those trips maintained a connection with my mother's family that gave me a strength and a perseverance that I carried with me. It was in Ohio that I began to see that I didn't have to work so hard to fit in.

Chapter Twelve

WHEN MY MOTHER AND I RETURNED HOME FROM Ohio after that first visit, our cozy apartment seemed empty and isolated. My sister returned from staying with Dave and as the weather turned cooler the three of us would sit together in front of the television, watching American football and eating supper. For the Sunday night game we would usually have a frozen microwave dinner of turkey with gravy and mashed potatoes. The small pouch of vivid red cranberry sauce always seemed vaguely celebratory, if slightly lurid. The steaming meal in its microwave tray would be set on a flimsy metal dinner stand in front of the living room recliners. (We still loved the Steelers and that year cheered on Louis Lipps to a Pro Bowl season, but it was a disappointing finish for our beloved Steel Curtain.)

I spent the first few days of fall with my grandparents. My dad was traveling, so it was just the three of us in their huge, luxurious apartment. The opulent, crushing silence of their place was head-spinning after Ohio's rowdy and cramped camaraderie. Their lifestyle suddenly appeared to me as wasteful and unfair. Whereas before I had been dazzled by the elegant beauty, I was now struck by the ugly disparity. My grandfather hadn't been feeling well, so he was home more than usual over that weekend. Holed up in his office, he worked, read the newspaper and took his meals on a tray. My grandmother preparing, delivering, collecting and washing up after each meal. Although I never dreamed of entering his office, I sometimes watched him through the crack in the door as he worked. Having just spent time with my family in Ohio, it finally dawned on me that race might be the reason he didn't like me. I'd always known he didn't approve of my parents' marriage and had some ancient grievances with my mother that she still ruminated over, but it was only after that visit to Ohio that I started to suspect that race could be a factor in why he didn't approve of my mother and me. Although he had become more friendly with me over the years, we had never been close and he never mentioned my mother by name. The fact that our race might have played a part was a jarring realization that suddenly made me look at both of my grandparents in a different light. My grandmother had always been someone I relied on and trusted, but now I felt betrayed by her and newly furious for my mother. I realized how naive I had been and felt foolish for not seeing the situation for what it was. Why hadn't my mother told me? All these years I had been forced to guess and wonder why the two women I loved most in the world seemed to hate each other. The adult emotions I didn't understand but was forced to navigate with my mother and grandmother had been brutal. The two of them lashing out at one another through me all of these years had left a lasting impact. I had been trying to protect both my mother and grandmother, and it now seemed to me they were both liars. It was a realization that shook me and left an angry scar. The scales had suddenly fallen from my eyes and I could not go back.

After that visit I began to make excuses not to see my grandparents. This absence was painful because I couldn't help missing my grandmother even though I was angry with her. Contradictory emotions that were incredibly confusing. During this time away, my grandfather's health continued to decline and he would need a difficult open-heart surgery that winter. In the meantime, I began grade five at Hawthorne Public School, which was a new, progressive, alternative elementary school near our apartment. My mother had heard about a trial program being run out of the neighborhood school and immediately signed me up. I would once again have to make a new start with new friends.

★ ★ ★

I am lucky enough to have had a few exceptional public school teachers in my life. Grade five was one of those wonderful years. Our teacher, Peter—as he asked us to call him at the start of the year—was a gentle, bespectacled education rebel. On the first day of school he informed us we could put our desks anywhere in the class we liked, and we proceeded to do so. That day and for the rest of the year we moved and sorted and piled our desks as we saw fit. He taught us poetry, art history and math by getting us up and walking around the school, measuring and multiplying our steps or drawing the clouds. Peter watched our machinations with a wicked little smile and encouraged us to be bolder and more innovative. At one point in the middle of the year, a classmate who was interested in architecture brought in a cardboard box and asked if he could mount it on his desk. Peter thought it over for a minute and then agreed to the experiment. By the end of the year the entire class had set up a massive, teetering cardboard city on our desks. The desks were connected by paper towel tubes and ramps made out of cereal boxes. Tissue boxes were added as storage spaces for pencils and erasers. We had developed an intricate system to pass notes to each other that involved moving a toilet paper tube through tunnels and connected ramps with a string. We hung signs at the openings to our desks that informed our classmates when we were doing work and shouldn't be interrupted or if we were open to a chat. Peter gamely walked under and around our creations to get to the middle of the room and the rug where he now had to teach our lessons. He encouraged big ideas, and radical research and development to test them out.

During the spring of grade five, Peter called me over to his crowded desk one morning and told me that some local producers were developing a new kids television series called *OWL/TV*, based on *OWL* magazine. The magazine was a kids' publication with a focus on outdoors and wildlife that Peter kept in the classroom. They had approached a few teachers at several public schools to select students who might like to try out for the show. He gave me a sheet of paper with a time and address on it and told me to give it to my mom if I was interested. I shoved it in my jeans pocket and forgot about it until my mom found it a few days later while doing laundry. She asked if I wanted to check it out and I figured I'd give it a shot.

That weekend my mom and I drove to a small studio in the city's east end in the yellow Volkswagen Rabbit my mother had inherited after the split from Dave. It was a stick shift that was rusting, had pretty bald tires and was on its last legs. We normally took the subway everywhere we went, but the audition was on the other side of the city and my mom had decided to take the car. We pulled up to a low-rise building hunkered down in an industrial area near the lake. My mother and I signed in and then found a seat in the waiting room with a bunch of other kids my age. We sat in silence staring at each other until we were called in to another room in groups of four. Inside, a young guy in a baseball cap and with a bored expression sat with an old-school video recorder on a tripod. There were a couple of older women sitting behind a large table at the back of the windowless room, quietly conferring with each other. A young, enthusiastic woman approached us with a smile and seemed to be in charge of herding and encouraging us. Once she had us lined up, the cameraman flipped a switch that activated a red light on the camera and we said our names and what school we were coming from. "Anais Granofsky, Hawthorne Public School." Then the young woman called out a few improvised games and situations and the four of us laughed nervously and tried to keep up with her prompts. At this point I was still a pretty outgoing kid with adults and from my days on Fakeer's communes, quite used to playacting like a fool. I had howled at the moon while dancing around a bonfire with my dad's naked friends covered in dirt. Pretending I was at the zoo or shopping in a grocery store wasn't going to throw me. I hammed it up in front of the camera and the women behind the table laughed. It was immediately intoxicating, this sudden ability to get the adults in the room to pay attention. I realized this was a space where you were rewarded for shifting who you were to please the adults. After all of my experiences code-switching for my grandparents, parents and friends, it turned out I was rather good at it. Once finished, we were all thanked for coming in and then released back to our moms, who were waiting for us expectantly.

We were living in the west end of Toronto at the time, which was still pretty rough, but the east end of the city, where the studio was, had several large, beautiful beaches lining Lake Ontario. Since we were all the way across town and we had the car, my mom suggested we go to the beach and get an ice cream. My mother was not a confident driver. She had taken to putting a large cardboard sign in the back window that read *SLOW DRIVER!! GO AROUND!*, the words written in black magic marker. She was especially bad at hills with the stick shift. If we came to a red light that happened to stop us on an incline, my mother would become very, very nervous. The car would lurch back and forth as she tried to keep us in gear, swearing and starting to freak out. "Girl, you've gotta go tell them!" Her fingers gripping the steering wheel. "Mom! Come on!" Inevitably, she would force me out of the car where I would stand, refusing to move until I eventually gave in to my mother's hysterical admonitions. Turning, I would ruefully walk downhill in the rain, snow, sleet, sun to the car idling behind us. The other car's driver would watch my approach suspiciously and only roll down their window a crack. "Hi, my mom's a bad driver and she wants you to move back so she doesn't hit you." They would normally look confused. "Trust me, she's going to roll." Then they would shrug their shoulders and decide to steer away from trouble. I would get back in the car and we would lurch into first gear and slowly, excruciatingly grind our way to the top of the incline.

But on this sunny day we drove to the Beaches without incident, bought ice cream cones and sat by the boardwalk looking out over Lake Ontario. I was still on a high from the audition, adrenaline coursing through me and a giddy feeling in my chest. I couldn't wait to tell my dad about this unexpected world I had stumbled into. He had always loved theater and I knew he was going to get a kick out of this. That day on the boardwalk, as my mom and I watched people out for a Sunday stroll, she would make up stories about their lives. If they were happy or sad, what they did for a living, their secret regrets. She would point. "Just look at their shoes. You can always tell what kind of person someone is by their shoes. People might try and fool you with how they dress and behave, but their shoes will tell you the truth."

★ ★ ★

By this point I hadn't seen my grandparents in close to a year. I had initially been avoiding them, but that was made easier when my grandfather developed post-op complications that kept him convalescing down in Florida. My grandparents ended up spending most of the year at their home in West Palm Beach while my grandfather recovered from an infection after another heart-valve surgery, a complication of the rheumatoid fever he had suffered as a child in Romania. Although my ardor had cooled significantly, I had begun to really miss Shirley. She had tried to keep in touch over the months we spent apart and had even invited me to come visit them in Florida. That spring, for March Break, my grandmother sent a plane ticket so that I could fly to see them.

I was nervous to see Shirley because I didn't know how it would feel to be with her again. Although I tried not to show it to my mom, I couldn't deny how excited I was to go on a trip. It had been a tough year. My dad had been traveling to Rajneeshpuram a lot and my sister was now with Dave for half the week, so it was back to my mom and me on our own. I needed the break, but I had decided that I would remain unwavering and cool to my grandmother after my earlier suspicions. I girded myself and flew down to my grandparents' winter home. But when I came off the plane, Shirley was so glad to see me that I couldn't help yielding to her efficient love, relieved to be in her stabilizing presence. We quickly fell into a comfortable routine, waking and eating breakfast and then going for a brisk walk around the neighborhood. When we returned, my grandfather would join us for a swim in the pool and then read the newspaper. With nothing else to do, I eventually joined him. Phil and I sat side by side in matching chaise lounges by the kidney-shaped pool and read the *Florida Tribune* or the *Palm Beach Jewish Weekly News*. I was resolute in remaining angry at him, but my grandfather seemed different on that trip. He had always been a diminutive man with an outsized, commanding presence, but his recent serious health problems had diminished him considerably. He seemed so much smaller and older than I remembered. And he also seemed more up for a laugh. Sharing a comic strip with me in the morning funnies or commenting on a particularly funny article in the newspaper we were reading. The irony was that my grandfather loved tanning himself to a crisp. By the end of his trip he had dutifully sunned himself to a deep chestnut brown that was darker than I was. He also began to join us for breakfast instead of having it on a tray in his room. My grandfather and I would sit on the balcony while my grandmother served us in an apron and that coral lipstick, perfectly applied.

Phil and I unexpectedly began to chat with each other during those early morning meals by the ocean, talking easily together for the first time. We'd sit in the morning sunshine looking out over the water while eating sliced tomatoes by the bushel with a little kosher salt. He loved sliced tomatoes, always giving my grandmother a slight pat on the tuchus in appreciation when she laid down a fresh plate. We talked about when he was a kid and he told me stories about the anti-Semitism he faced as a young man in the forties. After he had graduated high school with honors in mathematics, his father had wanted him to enroll in the chemical engineering course at the University of Toronto. Soon after the school year began, he told me the five Jewish students in the course were called down to the dean's office. The dean informed them that no matter how good their grades might be, none of them were going to be able to find a job in the field when they graduated. Discouraged and full of a driving ambition, my grandfather quit his studies and joined his father's business. He fought and scraped for everything he had built, starting a business in his parents' garage and growing it machine by machine, client by client through sheer force of will. He was proud of his success and enjoyed talking with me about the early days of the company, although he was thoroughly surprised at my interest. "You really want to hear about this?" "Yah, sure." I nodded. "Your father always hated talking about the business. His mother knew how to talk with him. I tried, but I never knew how to get through to him." He looked over at me and shook his head. Then he reached out and patted my hand gently, looking away. "I guess it works out in the end."

I had always been afraid of him; he was so inscrutable. But at that moment, I realized we weren't so different. He too had experienced hardship, prejudice and poverty. He looked over at me and we took each other in as if for the first time. It was confusing to feel so angry with someone and love them too. It was the first time I felt some kind of love for him and loved by him in a way. He never asked, but I forgave him after that for not wanting my mother and me.

Their past grievances were not mine, and I couldn't hold on to them any longer.

* * *

THE next time I saw him was that spring at the Atlantic Packaging picnic. After our time in Florida, I was excited to spend the day with him. Every year my grandfather threw a huge picnic and company party for his employees. For the event, Atlantic took over the massive parking lot at their main production plant on a wide street in an industrial park north of the city. Balloons, cotton candy machines, hot dog carts and games were set up and food handed out for free all day. I pulled up with my grandmother and grandfather in their salmon Cadillac, giddy with delight; other than Christmas, it was my favorite day of the year.

Every employee at Atlantic was there with their families: the truck drivers who hauled the eighteen-wheelers, the machine operators and press print controllers, the secretaries and the front office staff all gathered for the event with their families and co-workers. Most people didn't know who I was. There were quite a few Black and brown employees and front office staff, and it seemed like most people assumed I was one of the staff kids, so I spent the day in complete anonymity roaming the party. Along with the food and balloons, there were foot races. I loved the races. After lunch everyone headed over to the grassy field beside the parking lot where temporary lanes had been set up with ropes and a ribbon across the finish line. Every age group of kid participated, from the youngest to the oldest, and it was the main event of the afternoon. All the adults gathered around the perimeter of the field and cheered the kids on—my grandfather, wearing a three-piece suit and tie in the heat, standing at the finish line ready to hand out medals to the victors. I remember waiting for my age to be called with my heart pounding and a fierce determination in my gut. That medal was going to be mine, and my grandfather was going to give it to me in front of everyone. I was going to win this bloody race or die trying. When the pop gun went off those other kids didn't know what hit them; I won by a mile. After the race I stood grinning ear to ear, fairly bursting with pride as my grandfather placed a red-ribboned plastic gold medal around my neck. Then I turned and hugged him hard, arms squeezed around his waist, my face buried in his suit buttons. The people around us laughed at what they presumed was an employee's kid hugging the boss, but I didn't care and hugged him tighter.

★ ★ ★

To my great surprise and delight, *OWL/TV* finally called as the grade-five school year was wrapping up. They booked me for a couple of small segments they were shooting called "Real Kids." I was going to be paid $100 for an afternoon of filming—a huge sum! "Real Kids" was essentially an expanded version of what we had done in the audition room. They brought a couple kids to a studio and filmed them in fun situations, playing with rabbits or making arts and crafts. Those clips would then be used as fillers between larger shows in the series.

I filmed a couple of different segments over the course of an afternoon and had a great time. I was a natural in front of the camera, willing to be outgoing and curious without looking stiff. By the end of the shoot I was sitting on the camera dolly looking through the lens and chatting with the crew. In those early days, I discovered that being on a set felt comfortable, a place I belonged. For the first time, I had something that was totally my own. In my other worlds, whether it was with my mother, father or grandmother, I had felt the imperative to shift who I was to accommodate the person I was with. It was similar on set. I was still required to use that particular set of skills, but now I could be in control. The code-switching was not a reaction; it felt proactive and exhilarating and I was getting paid! The ability to play a role came naturally, and it brought with it the full approval of the adults in the room. I was used to navigating adult spaces—I had often been the only kid in a roomful of adults—and I settled in on set easily. I immediately felt I had found the world in which my skills were most fully encouraged and rewarded. I was given $100 cash at the end of the day and my mom and I celebrated with a big combo-bucket of KFC and then used what was left to pay the heating bill. I'll never forget the feeling of paying that bill with the money I earned. I was so proud to help my mother out in such a tangible, grown-up way. It was not so long ago that being broke had threatened to destroy us. I hadn't been able to do anything about it then, but I could now.

★ ★ ★

SCHOOL ended at Hawthorne Public for the year, and with summer, a change in my social standing was ushered in. My experiences in Ohio, the trip with my grandparents and my time on set had shifted my confidence and given me something that I now carried with me rather than collected as I went along: an innate sense of belonging that translated into a new attitude with my peers, where I didn't feel I had to hide who I was anymore.

In the middle of the summer, *OWL/TV* called me in again to audition for an original series they were developing called *The Mighty Mites*. *The Mighty Mites* was a cartoon segment in *OWL* magazine about three friends who have the ability to shrink down in size and go exploring in the natural world. It was a mix of *Honey, I Shrunk the Kids* and a PBS nature show. They were adapting the cartoon into a live-action series and wanted a diverse cast for the adventurous entomological friends. The night before the audition the production office faxed a script to the corner store, and I spent the entire evening studying the lines. Earnestly repeating them to the mirror in our small bathroom. The next morning my mom, sister and I fired up the rusted Volkswagen and drove across town for the audition. At the studio, my mom signed me in. I had my picture taken with a Polaroid camera and was then sent alone to wait in a room full of other kids rehearsing their lines. My heart was jack-hammering in my chest and my sweaty palms gripped the script. I was finally called into the room with two other kids, and we lined up and gave our names and schools. This audition was much bigger than the first one I had breezed through. In the room, we were now taking direction from a casting agent who organized the scenes. We had to say the memorized dialogue as we mimed ducking away from flying beetles and maneuvering around blades of grass. It was all very grand and exciting and I took to it right away, an enthusiastic participant in this make-believe world full of adventure. I was actually a little disappointed when the audition came to an end. They thanked us for our time and we left and I rejoined my mom and sister in the hallway. As we walked through the parking lot, my mom quizzed me on how it went. Even though I had loved every minute and wanted the job so badly my stomach hurt, I downplayed it. Shrugging off her inquiries as we got in the hot car. There was no reason to do this; she was excited for me and I was hopeful. But over the years, to protect my mother's feelings, I had gotten used to telling her very little and it was now my default response. As I got older, I told her less and less just as she wanted to know more.

On the way home our yellow Volkswagen Rabbit finally died with a shuddering wheeze and we rolled to a stop. We ended up leaving it by the side of the road, the *SLOW DRIVER!! GO AROUND!* sign still taped in the back window. My mom, sister and I took the streetcar the rest of the way across town and arrived home late, hungry and exhausted. As we walked in the door the phone rang and my mother answered it. The production company was calling to let us know I had gotten the part of Sophie Mite. With our ears to the receiver my mother and I began jumping up and down in silent celebration. The producer continued: "You'll be faxed the contract for a thousand dollars for the week of work." Our jaws dropped, a huge sum to both of us. "The series is filming outside of Ottawa on a professional sound stage. Transportation and hotel fees will be paid by the production. Is she available?" "Yes! Yes!" I immediately screamed, and after hanging up, my mom, sister and I danced around the room. The next morning we proudly walked down to the landlord's office to pay our rent early for the next month.

* * *

I spent the week I turned twelve, in the summer of 1985, shooting the *Mighty Mites* in downtown Ottawa. My mother had to work the week I was shooting so she stayed in Toronto and I traveled with the production on my own. The cast stayed at what seemed like a fabulously fancy hotel, although it was just a Marriott by the side of Highway 417. The two other actors and I were looked after by a chaperone from the production company who basically let us run wild in the hotel and order whatever room service we wanted. In the mornings the cast was picked up and driven to set where we were fitted in our explorer costumes. High-waisted khaki shorts, a tucked-in safari shirt and a white safari hat. It was all incredibly glamorous for a knock-kneed, bucktooth kid with a curly mullet on her first professional job. The acting was horrendous and the show was ludicrous, but it felt like I was killing it. We shot for a week on a large empty soundstage in front of a blue screen that they would be filling with wildlife. I spent the days hanging from a harness in front of the massive blue screen, pretending to swim underwater while investigating a water bug. Or bravely pushing through imaginary grass on a savanna to look for a grasshopper. At night, the other two actors and I hung out in our hotel rooms and ordered candy from room service and watched as much television as we wanted. I was hooked.

On set, I became friends with the director, a thirtysomething Brit who was fun to work with and had a wicked sense of humor. When we would break for lunch, he would sit with the cast in the lunch room and joke around and tell stories. On the last day of the shoot he told me about a kids series he and his partner were producing back in Toronto. It was going to be a gritty series based on real kids and they wanted local kids to try out for the roles. He gave me the address and encouraged me to come by when they had the auditions. The show was called *Kids of Degrassi Street*.

* * *

In September, back in Toronto, I started grade six at Hawthorne, again in Peter's class. Peter was as rowdy and unconventional as ever and I loved his educational anarchy and considered him a friend. Now that I was a "television actor" I had surprisingly become a grade-six powerbroker. When *The Mighty Mites* aired on *OWL/TV* shortly after the start of the school year, I became a genuine neighborhood celebrity.

My dad had returned to Toronto for a long spell after the Ranch in Oregon had spectacularly collapsed. Amid accusations of assault, fraud and even attempted murder, Rajneeshpuram had been raided by the FBI, and Bhagwan, now known as Osho, had fled the state in a private jet. He was arrested the next morning on a North Carolina air-strip wearing a fur hat and coat and eventually plead guilty to two federal felonies. After paying $400,000 in fines he promptly left for India, where he would remain for the rest of his life. The Ranch in Oregon was eventually shuttered in ignominy and the sannyasins dispersed. My dad returned to Toronto disillusioned with the Ranch's leadership but determined to remain connected to his master and the group of sannyasins he had established in Canada. Now that he was back in the city I happily began to spend weekends with him again. My mom used the nights I was away and enthusiastically went back to school to complete a one-year degree in social work at George Brown College. She began to work for the Toronto District School Board, helping new immigrants adjust to the Canadian school system and find a job in their new country, a service that was similar to the one at the YMCA that had saved us all those years ago. After all this time, she had finally managed to combine her interests in community activism and education. My grandmother was thrilled with my newfound celebrity, and although she had absolutely no understanding about the television acting world, she knew the value of bringing home a check. She proudly encouraged me to go where this new career was leading.

* * *

THE *Degrassi* audition process took place in a shabby little house near Pape and Queen East. This time, I rode the streetcar across town by myself. I had begun to take public transit to get between my mom's and dad's places and I enjoyed the freedom it gave me. I didn't have to rely on anyone to get me where I wanted to go. I had been told I was going to be there all day, so I packed a lunch and some snacks. From the outside the house didn't look like much, but inside, the ground floor had been opened up into a large empty room. Once I checked in by the front door, I joined about twenty other kids between the ages of eleven and thirteen who were nervously sitting on fold-out chairs that lined the putty-gray walls. The kids were of every different background, race and culture, and we all sat silently sizing each other up. A blond, curly-haired woman with glasses came out of a back room and introduced herself. She was Linda Schuyler, one of the creators of the series. She seemed warm and smart and had the energy of a teacher, which she'd once been. She introduced my director, Kit Hood, to the rest of the kids and informed us that they were going to lead the auditions.

The rest of the day was like a boot camp for kid actors. We were divided up into smaller groups and Linda and Kit took us through several improv exercises just to get warmed up. They would call out scenarios and each group would have to play the scene out. There was a lot of nervous laughter and some genuinely hilarious moments. Later, we had to perform scenes that were written in script form and manage to get some rudimentary staging down. I had never been to an acting class in my life, but I had just finished *The Mighty Mites* and the auditioning process felt natural by now. I loved connecting with the other kids and always enjoyed getting a laugh out of the adults in the room. At the lunch break all the kids ate sitting on the front porch, getting to know each other. Almost everyone had brought their lunches from home, and the curries, spanakopita and bologna sandwiches were all unwrapped and devoured while we joked and one-upped each other. It was wonderful to be surrounded by such a diverse mix of kids. Everyone was completely unique and it made me feel seen and celebrated not in spite of my radical differences but because of them.

By early afternoon, Linda and Kit thanked us for our time and said they'd be in touch. I rode the streetcar home elated and exhausted. That week I went back to school, where we wrapped up for the Christmas holidays and Peter threw the class a big winter solstice party. I celebrated Hanukkah with Phil and Shirley at their house with my dad, my aunts and uncle and their kids, my six cousins. We sat at a long, beautifully set table and ate a feast that my grandmother had spent days preparing. On New Year's Eve, my mom, sister and I rang in 1986 together eating McDonald's and watching the Dick Clark New Year's special on television. All along, I anxiously waited to hear back about the audition.

Early in the new year, I got a call from the *Degrassi* production office letting me know I had gotten a role on the series that would shoot in the spring. I was cast as one of the smaller characters in only a few episodes of the incredibly low-budget production, but I was thrilled. I had finally found a place where all of the parts of myself could be brought to bear. I couldn't know it at the time, but it would become one of the most important jobs of my life.

Chapter Thirteen

SEVERAL MONTHS LATER I SHOT MY EPISODES FOR *Kids of Degrassi Street* over the course of a couple weeks. Early in the morning my mom or dad would drop me off at the small production office on Degrassi Street in the city's east end. There were about ten kids who made up the show's cast, and after a few days hanging out around the set we slowly became friends. On set we wore our own clothes and didn't have our hair or our makeup done. Linda and Kit wanted us to look like real kids dealing with real issues—pimples, bad haircuts and all. The crew was small and everyone was young and inexperienced, but they were driven and passionate. It was like another boot-camp for low-budget filmmaking and I was completely smitten.

We completed shooting the six-episode series in a whirlwind couple of weeks and I then returned to school to finish up my last semester of grade six with Peter. I ended the school year on a high, and Peter graciously held our small graduation at his home in the Annex. He had seen something in me I hadn't even seen in myself, and I was incredibly grateful for the opportunity he had given me. I was sad to be leaving such an academically exciting class but was also looking forward to grade seven and junior high. That summer, after airing a season of *Kids of Degrassi*, Linda and Kit decided to move the series up to junior high, along with the actors who were naturally getting older. They changed the name to *Degrassi Junior High* and we had to audition again for new roles in the new series. I had become a bit of an old hand at the auditioning process and I walked in ready to strut my stuff. I was thirteen and feeling pretty good about myself. I had grown out my mullet, and braces had straightened out my buck teeth. The auditions were an intensive two-week workshop that was a mix of improv, acting class and group discussions about topics that were important to us. During the discussions, the head script writer, Yan Moore, a bearded, bespectacled man with a kind countenance, would scribble furiously into his notebook. Nodding and smiling when one of us would say something he liked or wanted to circle back to. At one point, I was auditioning for the role of a rebellious badass and I had to do a scene where I was smoking. Incredibly, they had a pack of cigarettes in case one of us decided we were a method actor. I had never smoked before but I figured it would lend some gravitas to my performance.

During my scene, in front of everyone, I lit the smoke and only realized I had ignited the wrong end of the cigarette when the filter caught fire. Wanting to keep the mojo going, I inhaled and immediately coughed so hard my eyes turned red and I almost threw up. I didn't get the role. But I did get the role of Lucy Fernandez, a feminist firebrand with a penchant for sparkly scarves, and we began filming *Degrassi Junior High* in the summer of 1986. It wasn't obvious then, but the show would go on to become a cultural phenomenon and a huge international hit. It was an awards behemoth that was celebrated for telling groundbreaking stories about a diverse, multicultural cast of characters. Our different backgrounds and unique perspectives were about to make us stars. But it was still early in that first year and I was just trying to find my way.

★ ★ ★

THE set was a real school in Etobicoke. Vincent Massey Public School was on a small side street of modest bungalows at the western edge of the city. The production had rented out the entire school, including the library, cafeteria, gym and all the classrooms, for the summer to shoot the series. The morning call time was usually the crack of dawn at the Playing With Time production offices on Queen Street

East. The cast would gather on the dirty sidewalk as the sun came up and wait to be bussed to the location. Several long yellow school buses would pull up and the cast would sleepily board and make the thirty-minute ride to set. No seatbelts, kids jumping seat to seat and goofing off while a production assistant white-knuckled the massive yellow school bus along the Gardiner Expressway to get us to set by our call time. The production was a bit bigger than *Kids of Degrassi Street* but still a pretty low-budget endeavor. We brought our own clothes and picked the outfits our characters would wear. We did our own makeup and hair, and very few of us had much professional experience. The acting was rudimentary at best, but the scripts were ambitious and tackled subjects that had never been discussed in a kids show before.

The cast of kids quickly became a roving band of buddies at work, everyone hanging out together in the library or lying out on the soccer field on shooting breaks. The last time I had felt part of a group like that, beyond family, was at Adventure Playground and the YMCA daycare. My mom and I had moved around so much that I didn't ever get a chance to make friends and keep them for long. I was always the new kid trying to break into a group that had been well established before my arrival. Here, we were all new, we came from completely different backgrounds and families, but we had acting in common. It bonded us very quickly and made it feel like we had known each other for longer than we actually had. There were about ten actors who were the main characters, a group of smaller characters and then the kids who were background actors. The background performers never had lines but were always walking in the hall or sitting in the classroom in the background of scenes. When we weren't filming, we would all play board games, read or flirt with each other in the school library. Production had outfitted the library with couches and tables pulled in from other classrooms to house the thirty-odd pubescent teens. The library became the cast's main hangout area between filming scenes. If our character had a scene coming up, it's where we would run lines with the other actors and work on the staging before going on set. Set was usually hot and crowded and in one of the small classrooms or the hallway. I quickly learned to dodge lighting stands, the camera dolly tracks and sandbags. Most of the time you were mainly required to hit your mark and find your light while remembering your lines. I was ridiculously happy.

Read-throughs of the script and rehearsals were on the weekend. The cast that was appearing in the episode would gather at the production office for a table read. We would read through the script and then have a frank discussion around what felt authentic and what didn't. Linda, Kit and Yan always listened to what the kids had to say with interest, scribbling down lines that would often end up in the show later. They gave us a space to try on our own opinions about what it meant to be a kid and the issues we felt strongly about. It was incredibly empowering to be listened to and to have your creative ideas acted upon at that age. For the first time I began to understand that my differences—straddling poverty and wealth, being Black and Jewish and the daughter of a hippie father and a conservative mother—gave me power. My perspective was not only welcome but sought out and celebrated. I had begun to extract who I was from the people who had raised me and was starting to find my own place in the world. One where I didn't have to bend to the will of my family.

This inevitably began to cause conflict at home. I was thirteen, making a bit of money and definitely feeling myself. This new world was mine and I didn't want to share it with my mom. We began to fight and I quickly shut her out, refusing to emotionally support her any longer. Because we were filming from Monday to Friday and rehearsing on the weekend, I also hadn't seen my grandparents that summer. As I became busier with the series, I began to see them less, instead choosing to spend the weekends with my new friends. I would now visit my grandparents for a swim with my dad or at the holidays, but I stopped going for sleepovers. My grandmother continued to invite me to Sunday nights at the Primrose but I once again made excuses not to go. I didn't want to be who they expected me to be anymore.

My dad spent most of the summer of that year at the commune in Quebec. Usually I would have gone with him but this year I remained in the city to work. I was disentangling myself from everything I had known and loved and striking out on my own. In the past, I had willingly contorted who I was to fit the situation and I was now refusing to play my part at home. My life was my new friends and acting and I threw myself into the show with a fervor. I had found my people and something that I was good at and I didn't look back.

* * *

AFTER that first season of *Degrassi*, things really began to fall apart at home. When I started to make some real money, it changed the dynamic with my mom. I was now paying our rent and most of the bills, and although my mom was incredibly grateful for this help, she was also starting to resent the freedoms it was giving me. It surprised us both that my success had also granted me a kind of equalizing power and with it a sense of entitlement. I had my own money, I was paying the rent and I didn't need to ask her for anything financially. I had a job that I loved and my acting friends, who were the center of my social life. She was no longer the sun that I orbited around, and the gravitational pull that I had felt all my life was waning. I now realize that I was also incredibly angry at her and resentful whenever I perceived that I was being pressured to parent my parent. She continued to need my reassurance, but I now vehemently refused to give it to her. These were natural teenage issues that were exacerbated by the fact that I was earning close to what my mother was making at her job. The fights at home became more heated and vicious and I began spending as much time out of the house as I could. I had begun high school and took my driver's test the day I turned sixteen. With my own money I bought a second-hand beater convertible and began driving myself to work and school and sleeping away from my house.

* * *

THE more I was away, the more grasping my mother became when I was home. The foundational interdependence of our relationship, something that had always felt unshakable, had become untenable. Mom and Ma. An emotional weight that I became more and more determined to shake. After a particularly nasty fight, in which my mother accused me of being an ungrateful rich little bitch (which, to be honest, I probably was), I packed a few clothes and belongings and moved into my father's house on Brunswick Avenue in the Annex neighborhood. He had bought a skinny Victorian on a charming, quiet street near the University of Toronto and Chinatown, but was very rarely there. I often had the place to myself and quickly filled it with friends. My mother didn't speak to me for six months after I moved out, and after a few times trying to call her I stopped reaching out. I would not bend to her needs any longer. I was now sixteen and essentially on my own.

As I became an older teenager, and especially after I moved into his house, Fakeer and I got along like gang-busters. I was helping to pay the bills in his house, too, so I didn't need much from him. He was gone a lot of the time, and when he was home, he put very little pressure on me to conform to much of anything. An extroverted teen-ager's dream parent. When he was home, he would host Kundalini meditations with other sannyasins in our living room. A large group of adults dressed in red and orange, hugging, dancing and singing under a huge black-and-white portrait of Osho that hung over the fireplace. Osho's black beard had turned gray over the years, his face still hand-some, his eyes alight with a mischievous look that used to follow me across the room. At night my dad would some-times have a large group of friends over for loud music-filled dinners. All of us crowded into our small kitchen eating potluck quiches and quinoa salads, discussing politics and philosophy. I was treated as an adult and could stay or come and go as I pleased. Some mornings when he was in town and I was at home we would make breakfast together and eat at the kitchen table, the back doors open onto the small, tangled garden and paint-chipped garage. We would sit together listening to the birds or talk about his travels or my work, which he loved hearing about. I had forgiven him many years ago on that beach for having left when I was younger. And as a teenager I was much more willing to accept his absences than my mother's neediness. I was now craving independence and he gave it to me. He didn't ask permission to live his life as he pleased and he gave me the freedom to forge my own path.

I still saw my grandparents, but much less regularly throughout those years. Every so often we went to the Primrose Club for Sunday night dinner like we used to. Pulling up in my grandfather's Cadillac, the gloved doormen helping my grandmother out of the car. She would check her fur at the downstairs coat check and we would walk up the grand stairs to the glittering dining room. The city still spread out below the floor-to-ceiling windows, white tablecloths and waiters who greeted my grandparents by name. My grandparents still cut quite a figure crossing the dining room to their table as I followed. Phil was physically diminished but, as always, the captain of industry, while my grandmother was still glamorous. Once seated, I still ordered the matzo ball soup, brisket and Jell-O, and filled up on challah coated in the carved balls of salted butter the waiters placed on the table. But an interesting thing started to happen as the show's influence grew, and my fame along with it. Older men and women would still approach my grandparents to talk business or a recent donation, but now their grandkids would come along with them. After introductions were made, the grandkids would ask for an autograph or to take a picture, and soon I had more people approaching our table than my grandfather did. I could see his surprise as these interactions grew more frequent, a realization of my sudden stature starting to creep into his eyes. My grandmother couldn't contain her pride, she would plotz to every person within earshot that her granddaughter was on television.

My acting career had done something unexpected to my relationship with my grandparents as well. Whereas with my mother that equalizing force had been destructive, with my grandparents it put me on a level that we all enjoyed. They basked in my relative fame, and my work gave me the space to drop the instinct to shape shift for them and just be who I was. Acting had given me the ability to stop acting when I was with my family. Degrassi had given me my own accomplishments that existed between all of the other worlds I had grown up in. Several years later the Primrose Club was sold, torn down and eventually turned into condominiums.

★ ★ ★

AFTER not speaking for months after I moved out, my mother and I slowly began to reconcile our fractured relationship. She had been furious when I moved into my father's house and saw it as a great betrayal. I was angry with her for leaning on me so heavily when I was younger and continuing to demand emotional reassurances as I got older. I left vowing not to give an inch. But as the months went on, we became better at setting our boundaries and laying less blame at each other's doorstep. After I forced her to relinquish control of me, she began to pay attention to her own dreams and aspirations again. I was still paying her rent and she was working steadily, so she was more financially stable than she had ever been. My sister was getting older and still splitting her time between our mom and Dave, and my mom suddenly had time on her hands. A strange sensation after so many years of hustling, crashing and rebuilding. We again began to look for that sense of connection that ran between us, and it was still there. Like a lifeline. I never lived with her again but we began to speak regularly. Most Fridays I would bring groceries to her place and cook dinner with Lea while she rubbed her feet and told us about her day. My sister and I laughing at her outrageous tales with our arms wrapped loosely around each other. Holding on to that bond as tightly as we could. Our small family of women eventually settling around my mother's table for dinner.

★ ★ ★

THE following year my mother moved back to Ohio to finally be closer to her family. She settled on a pretty little apple farm and planted vegetable gardens that she harvested in the summer and pickled for the winter. I con-tinued acting through high school as the show grew to be an international hit. After those teenage years and into my twenties, I continued to forge new relationships with the adults who raised me. The adults who had failed me and disappointed me. Comforted me and took care of me. The people who I loved who had loved me the best they could. In my early twenties, after the show had really taken off, I moved to New York, which took me out of the geographic center of my family and placed me in a town where I didn't know anyone. This move was a turn-ing point for me: I carved out a space of my own where I could be my own person, and where I could eventually reflect on the past. In those years of my young adulthood and onward, I spent a lot of time working through my feelings and issues from childhood. But most importantly, I eventually had children of my own and saw my joy, fail-ings and disappointments as a parent, which gave me a better understanding and helped me heal.

All of these experiences have given me the gift of empathy. From titans of industry to a single mother try-ing to survive in the projects, to child stars navigating teen-age-hood: we were all just doing the best we could with what we had. Sometimes I think of my ancestors who crossed oceans, farmed fields and bore the brunt of racism and anti-Semitism. I wonder what they would think of my beautiful Canadian life. My husband, Craig, and I now have three children who inhabit their own complicated and wonderful worlds. The cast of *Degrassi* gets together every now and then when we gather at someone's home for a reunion, retelling tales and laughing mightily. My mother still lives and works on the apple farm in Ohio, surrounded by family. She never remarried and we remain very close. My father is still a rolling stone, happily traveling from one continent to another, living exactly how he pleases. He splits his time between Europe, the United States and Brazil. He's a beautiful rebel and one of my favorite people to be around. In 1995, my grandfather fulfilled a lifelong dream, helping to bring the Raptors basketball franchise to Toronto. He died the same year. And Shirley, my Bubby, just celebrated her ninety-eighth birthday. She had seven beloved grandsons after me, but I am her only granddaughter. She's one of my best friends, and I visit her every week. In those quiet moments, we hold hands, and she tells me how much she loves me.

★ ★ ★

OVER the years I've had the time to reflect on my childhood and what it might mean to the bigger story. In my search to find the center between poverty and wealth, Black and white, security and chaos, is there a larger lesson? With the world alight with voices along the whole constellation of discussions around identity, intersectionality and anti-Black racism, what is it that holds people back or sets them free? In the end, what is it that makes the foundational difference in our stories? In all of the tumult of those early years, I had to find the cultural, racial and lived experiences that existed among the people I loved. This was long before conversations on intersectionality were common, and there was no guide to finding a place for me in the middle. I came from two families, one white and one Black, that had both experienced systemic oppression spanning multiple generations and came out at opposite ends of the economic spectrum. Only to clash fiercely when they shared a child. Multigenerational trauma and oppression were shared by the sides of my family, but their diverging paths forced me to lead dual lives as a child.

It took many years, but I was finally able to find where I belonged in the center of two families, histories and experiences. The imbalance of wealth and poverty were stark, oppression and opportunity intertwined with historical injustices and lived oppression. My Jewish ancestors were able to live the immigrant dream of working their way out of poverty toward generational prosperity. Their connection to community, war-time drive and the ability to pass in the wider white world set them up for success. But they were not insulated from family trauma and despair. My mother's people were unable to break the bonds of poverty in a system that was built on their labor. They worked their whole lives but were not able to avoid the generational, systemic poverty that they were born into. But this did not keep them from grace and the love of family. So, what is it to live a good life? I talk about this often with my own children. The next generation must find their own way, as I have found mine.

Acknowledgments

THANK YOU TO MY PARENTS. MY GRANDPARENTS. MY AUNTS and uncles. My children and my husband. Your patience and encouragement is appreciated more than you know.